# EVIL
# BEYOND
# BELIEF

CONTEMPORARY PERSPECTIVES
ON PHILOSOPHY OF RELIGION

*Brendan Sweetman and Curtis L. Hancock, Series Editors*

# EVIL
# BEYOND
# BELIEF

## JAMES PETRIK

*M.E. Sharpe*
Armonk, New York
London, England

HUMANITIES

**Library of Congress Cataloging-in-Publication Data**

Petrik, James M.
    Evil beyond belief / James Petrik.
        p.  cm. – (Contemporary perspectives on philosophy of religion)
    Includes bibliographical references and index.
    ISBN 0-7656-0282-2 (hardcover : alk. paper)
    1. Good and evil. 2. Theodicy. I. Title. II. Series.

BT160.P45 2000
214—dc21                                                    00-021347

Printed in the United States of America

The paper used in this publication meets the minimum requirements of
American National Standard for Information Sciences
Permanence of Paper for Printed Library Materials,
ANSI Z 39.48-1984.

BM (c)    10    9    8    7    6    5    4    3    2    1

For Rachel, Matthew, and Helena — three very good reasons to believe there is a God.

# Contents

# Foreword

In the contemporary academy the widespread interest in the philosophy of religion has created a demand for new, more accessible studies for a new generation of students and nonspecialists. The questions and issues of philosophy of religion have never had more appeal and have never been more relevant than they are now: Does God exist? What is the correct relationship between religion and science? Why does God allow evil? Which world religion, if any, is true? What is the appropriate relationship between religion and morality? Is contemporary naturalism a serious threat to religious belief? And so on.

This series from M.E. Sharpe, "Contemporary Perspectives on Philosophy of Religion," is aimed at introducing such topics in an accessible and fresh way, especially for undergraduate students. The books are intended primarily for undergraduate courses in philosophy of religion, and all will be written by experts in the field. However, because of the widespread popularity of the philosophy of religion in contemporary thought, the books in the series will likely have a wider appeal and should find a place also in those many introductory and advanced courses—in both philosophy and religion—that deal in some significant way with philosophy of religion-related issues.

In the field there is currently no series of textbooks aimed primarily at undergraduates and nonspecialists, and this series aims to remedy this deficiency. It is our hope that over time not only will the books in the series become standard textbooks but will also be recognized for making significant contributions to our overall understanding of the issues in the philosophy of religion.

Curtis L. Hancock
Brendan Sweetman
*Series Editors*

# Acknowledgments

Though this work certainly has a good many shortcomings, none of them is the result of a lack of support and assistance from others. Among those who read the manuscript in whole or part and provided me with valuable commentary are Curtis Hancock, John Petrik, Donald Borchert, Philip Schneider, Franklin Scott, Helen Petrik, Arthur Zucker, and Lynn Petrik. Brendan Sweetman deserves special mention for the painstaking scrutiny he brought to bear on this work. His philosophical criticisms were consistently to the point. His comments on my prose made me realize I'd gone semicolon happy. Thanks to Daphne Hougham for her excellent job of copyediting, and to Eileen Maass and Esther Clark who shepherded this work through its various stages of production. I am also indebted to Peter Coveney, the philosophy and religion editor at M.E. Sharpe. He was a consistent source of encouragement and never carped at my wanting to make just one more revision, for the seventeenth time. Finally, I'd like to thank my wife Lynn, not simply for the ways she has helped me see this project to completion, but also for putting up with me for the past nine years.

# Introduction

June 15, 1896, was a day of festival in the Japanese ports of Kamaishi and Yoshihama. They were still celebrating at seven in the evening when the earth moved. It was a moderate quake followed by a series of mild aftershocks, the result of a submarine fault giving way some 100 miles or so to the west, on the western side of the Japan Trench. By Japanese standards it wasn't much; enough to get one's attention but nothing that would dampen the festivities under way. It was twenty minutes after this unremarkable quake that the sea receded dramatically, exposing the ocean floor and stranding numerous fish. The significance of this development was lost on the townspeople, some of whom moved closer to witness the spectacle of nature. By the time they heard a hissing roar—some survivors likened it to the sound of a rainstorm—it was too late; the wall of water was upon them within moments. The tsunami's toll was enormous: 10,617 houses, 9,247 injured, and 27,122 dead. But this appalling physical toll wasn't the end of the suffering. Matters waxed perverse the following day. The town's fishing fleet had been well out to sea when the tragedy unfolded. As a tsunami can pass undetected on the open sea, the fishermen were completely unaware that anything was amiss. They were unaware, that is, until they neared harbor the next morning. It was then their vessels began plowing through water strewn with the wreckage of their homes and the bloated corpses of their relatives and friends.[1]

As remarkable as the Sanriku tsunami is in some respects, it is no less noteworthy for its lack of distinction. It is but one more episode in the long and cruelly rich history of the suffering that has befallen the earth's inhabitants. As far as natural disasters go, it is dwarfed by such calamities as the Pakistan cyclone of 1970, which had a death toll over 200,000, and the influenza epidemic of 1918, which killed over 500,000 in the United States alone. To find an earthquake that claimed five times as many lives as the Sanriku tsunami, one need go only twenty-seven years and fifty miles therefrom to the Great Kanto earthquake of 1923 that caused over 140,000 deaths in the Yokohama/Tokyo area. And it hardly needs mentioning that in this history the suffering inflicted by human beings on one another has rivaled that wrought by the afore-mentioned natural disasters.

I was reminded of this last fact in March of 1995. It was two months after my family and I had been fortunate enough to survive the Great Hanshin earthquake that claimed in excess of 6,000 lives and left large portions of the Japanese city of Kobe in ruins. Out of a kind of morbid curiosity I'd gathered back issues of the *Japan Times*. The front page of the newspaper issued on the day of the quake featured a large photo of a building with its entire facade torn away. Since the scene was typical of the kind of devastation that was routine after the earthquake, it took a moment for the puzzlement to set in. How was a morning newspaper able to run a photo of the devastation inflicted by an earthquake that had occurred at 5:45 A.M. on the very day that the paper was issued? It was only when I looked at the photo's caption that I realized my mistake. The photo was of the presidential palace in the Chechen capital of Grozny. It had been gutted by Russian artillery fire in the Chechen war of independence—a conflict that began in 1994, has claimed tens of thousands of lives, and has yet to be resolved. But much like the Great Hanshin earthquake, the Chechen war of independence will likely receive no more than fleeting notice in future histories of the twentieth century. When set in the context of the history of the suffering that humans have visited upon their own kind, it hardly catches one's attention. To see this, one need only consider that the onset of the Chechen conflict was roughly contemporaneous with the Rwandan civil war of 1994, a war in which over 800,000 Tutsi civilians—including a good percentage of children—were slaughtered in the genocidal mayhem that followed upon the assassination of the Hutu president, Juvenal Habyarimana. But simply quoting casualty counts is far from adequate to reveal the depths of suffering present in such tragedies. The devil, runs the overused bureaucrat's aphorism, is in the details. It's a maxim that takes on a chilling new light when one considers the specific ways in which some of the Tutsis were killed. As the physical stereotype portrays a Tutsi as tall and lean; the agents of genocide would sometimes cut their "haughty" victims down to size by using their machetes to hack off one foot and then the other, one hand and then the other, all while an appreciative throng jeered and hooted its approval.[2]

## The Problem of Evil

This discussion of various tragedies that have befallen human beings is meant to call attention to one point: Surveying but a tiny fraction of humanity's history is more than sufficient to illustrate that the world can be a very bad place to find oneself. So bad can it be that it is hard to take seriously the kind of counsel proposed in *Simple Abundance* by Sarah Ban Breathnach, a work of inspiration for women that had an impressive run in the marketplace. In this work we are cautioned that life "requires that we prepare ourselves for the inevitable times that try our souls," but are reassured that this goal can be "achieved with a comfort drawer." To help us get the hang of what a comfort drawer might be like, the author displays the contents of her own.

> Let's see what we find: a box of chocolate truffles; miniature (one-serving size) fruit cordials and after-dinner drinks; an aromatherapy bath treatment to promote serenity; various British decorating magazines (look for them at large cosmopolitan newsstands); a small vial of Bach's "Rescue Remedy," a homeopathic essence available at health food stores; a velvet herbal sleeping pillow to induce pleasant dreams; a satin eye mask to shut out distractions; rose-scented bubble bath and talc; old love letters tied with a silk ribbon; a scrapbook of personal mementos; a tin of fancy biscuits; and an assorted gift sampler of unusual teas.[3]

It is hard to read such advice and not conclude that a person whose problems could be pacified by a "comfort drawer" is a person who does not really understand how bad things can be and frequently are. What, one wonders, would be made of this advice by nineteenth-century women who held the dangerous occupation of extracting coal from mine shafts so cramped that the method of removal was for them to crawl while dragging buckets of coal that trailed behind them, attached by chain to a harness around the waist?[4] Viewed in this light, it is hard not to conclude that a person who would take seriously the recommended comfort drawer is a person who suffers from a kind of provincialism of privilege, an intellectual myopia that prevents one from comprehending how bad things can really be. But it is not my intent here to heap scorn upon the simple abundance philosophy. For one thing, it ought to be read with an eye to its intended audience and its intended aim, namely, helping fairly privileged Western women deal with the monotony and frustration attendant to meeting daily obligations. For another, as a fairly privileged Western man, I indulge in my own pacific flights into triviality and banality. The reason I have focused on the intellectual myopia behind the simple abundance philosophy is that I hold a view that many would judge to be guilty of precisely the same sort of blindness to how bad the world can be. I believe that the universe was created by an all-powerful, all-knowing, and all-loving God. That I am guilty of intellectual myopia in so believing is found, such critics would say, in the fact that one can cling to belief in God only by refusing to recognize all the evil that stands as evidence against the existence of an all-powerful, all-knowing, and all-loving Creator. These critics contend that the evil in the universe puts theism (belief in God) at odds with the evidence and thus at odds with reason. The point being made here is not simply that belief in God involves going beyond what reason can prove, for that is a point that many theists would grant. The charge being leveled is thus not simply that the theist cannot prove God's existence. It is, rather, that the theist is blind to the evident disproof of God's existence that one can find in the simple abundance of evil in the world. The charge that theists are guilty of such intellectual myopia is better known, among philosophers and theologians, as the problem of evil. This book is an introduction to and philosophical evaluation of this problem.

Given that I have already admitted to being a theist, where I shall come down on the issue is no secret; nonetheless, I will attempt to present the arguments of both theists and atheists as thoroughly and charitably as I can. This book is thus both a work *of* philosophy in which I defend certain conclusions and a work *on* philosophy in which many of the philosophical arguments on both sides of the issue are surveyed. Since it is meant as an introduction to the problem, I have attempted to present the arguments in language accessible to philosophical novices. Philosophical writing, like all specialized writing, has its share of technical terms, distinctions, and theories. While the use of such jargon can enhance economy of expression, it can substantially reduce a work's accessibility; not because those outside of philosophy lack the ability to follow it, but only because those outside of philosophy have not learned the philosopher's code. I have, therefore, attempted to keep my use of jargon to a minimum, and where I do use a technical term, I have tried to remember to explain it. In addition, to further serve the interests of accessibility, the remainder of this introduction will be devoted to explaining certain concepts, issues, and distinctions that are central to philosophical discussions of the problem of evil.

## Evil and Its Varieties

"Evil" is used frequently as a term of moral condemnation and thus as a term that applies only to morally corrupt beings and the morally corrupt things that they do. When used in this sense, it would simply be a confusion to describe the aftermath of a tornado as evil. The weather does what it does unconsciously and of physical necessity; therefore, it would be a mistake to think of such natural disasters as *morally* corrupt or evil. As should be evident from the sorts of tragedies listed in the opening paragraphs, "evil" as it figures in philosophical discussions of the problem of evil has a much wider sense than this. It applies no less to tragedies wrought by natural forces than it does to tragedies wrought by the free decisions of human beings. As used in discussions of the problem of evil, "evil" would cover roughly the same terrain as that commonly covered by "misfortune" or "tragedy." In this context, *evil* refers to whatever we think the universe would be better without and thus includes tragedies of both human and natural origin. The devastation of the Sanriku tsunami and the genocide in Rwanda were both great tragedies, and both are rightly classified as evil within the context of the problem of evil. Both challenge the theist to explain why a loving God would allow them to take place.

Even though natural disasters and atrocious human deeds count as evil within this context, the distinction between tragedies inflicted by human beings and tragedies inflicted by nature is a distinction of no small moment in philosophical treatments of the problem of evil. The former sort of evil is what philosophers call **moral evil** and the latter **natural evil**. The reason that the distinction between moral evil and natural evil has been thought important is that it is often alleged that the two kinds of evil call for very different accounts of why God would allow them. As will become evident in what follows, on my view there is significant overlap in the strategies that can be employed to reconcile belief in God with the existence of these very different sorts of evil; nonetheless, the overlap is far from complete and it will be well to bear the distinction between moral and natural evil in mind as you work through the arguments to come.

That the universe contains both moral and natural evils is not, of course, a problem for all forms of religious belief. For any religion that views the universe in which we find ourselves as the result of a conflict between a good deity and an evil deity of roughly comparable power, there is really nothing very puzzling about the fact that bad things happen.[5] No, evil is a special problem primarily for those theists who maintain that the supreme being behind the universe is good and loving, unrivaled in power, and having the knowledge needed to put the power to the service of the good ends dictated by love. The most extreme form of such theism and the one for which evil poses the greatest problem is also the one that will be assumed throughout this work. It conceives of God as an all-good (omnibenevolent), all-knowing (omniscient), and all-powerful (omnipotent) being who created the universe out of nothing (ex nihilo). There are three reasons that this will be the operative notion of God in this work. The first is that it is the conception that has dominated philosophical discussions of the problem of evil. The second is that it is a vision of God that is embraced by a great many people from a great many creeds.[6] The third is the following: If the problem of evil can be solved even under this extreme account of God's nature, then the prospects would likely be even more promising for solving it within a religion that has a more attenuated understanding of God's nature. Given that this account of God's nature will be assumed in the ensuing discussion, some brief remarks are in order about how the various components of this conception of God will be understood herein.

## God and God's Attributes

In saying that God is **omnibenevolent**, I mean that there is no instance in which either God's action or inaction is morally objectionable. It could never be truly said of such a perfectly good being that what He does is wrong. Nor could it be truly said that such a being's failure to do something is wrong. Put positively, it can be said that an omnibenevolent being's actions and inactions are exceptionlessly praiseworthy. Even saints have had their moral lapses. A morally perfect being can afford none without sacrificing its status as omnibenevolent.

In saying that God is **omniscient**, I mean that God knows all truth. This includes God's knowledge of all past, present, and future actualities as well as the laws and generalities that apply to the actual world. It also includes God's knowledge of possibilities and scenarios that might have been but are not. Such possibilities would include both different situations within the actual world (my wife might have married her high school sweetheart) and whatever worlds there might have been that have a different nature from the actual world (ones in which light is a liquid and trees can walk and talk). If we think of the total course of the universe's history as being akin to a complete game of chess, then we can say that God knows (1) all the moves that were actually made in the course of the game, (2) the rules of the game, (3) all the possible games of chess that might have been played, and (4) all other possible games—canasta, monopoly, baseball—that might have been created but were not. God knows, that is, everything there is to know. In addition to this positive knowledge of all-truth, omniscience also demands that God does not hold any beliefs that are false.

In saying that God is **omnipotent**, I mean that God can do all things. The rather vague term "things" in this definition is meant to cover logically possible states of affairs; that is, any description of what might be the case that is not internally contradictory. So God can turn water into wine, breathe life back into the dead, have manna fall from heaven, part the Red Sea, and sundry other astonishing deeds, but even God cannot make a square circle or make a triangle with only one angle or make a purple ball that has no color. While the former sort of marvelous events violate natural laws, laws that govern the way objects in the world behave, the latter sort violate the law of noncontradiction, for they entail that one and the same proposition is both true and false. Consider the case of God's making a purple ball that has no color. Insofar as purple is a color term, God's making a purple ball entails that the ball God makes has a color; therefore, the proposition that "there is a purple ball with no color" entails both that "the ball has color" and "the ball lacks all color"—a pair of propositions that is simply contradictory and thus cannot be affirmed together. I suspect that some readers will be wondering at this point just how omni God's omnipotence is. After all, having said that God can do all things, it may well be wondered why a logically contradictory state of affairs not be counted as describing some thing that God cannot do. Granted, the class of "things" was defined so as to cover only logically possible states of affairs; however, unless some account of this restriction is given, it seems to be a limitation on God's power by fiat and thus leaves open the door to a notion of power that is greater than omnipotence, superomnipotence perhaps—the power to do the logically impossible as well as the logically possible. There is, however, good reason for the restriction and good reason that an overwhelming majority of theistically inclined philosophers have been suspicious of the notion of superomnipotence.

To see what reason there is, attempt to construct in thought any one of the contradictory states of affairs mentioned above. Try, for instance, to really imagine what a square circle would be. Or try to imagine the colorless purple ball. After a few moments spent vainly thus, you might be inclined to concede that there really is no content that can be given to the states of affairs in question. Sure, you can imagine a circle, and yes, you can imagine a square, and you can even imagine the two figures set in a common spatial field. But what you cannot do is really conceive of what a square circle would be like, and that is because there is no conceivable state of affairs that corresponds to the unified description "square circle." The components of the description simply cannot go together. One and the same geometric figure cannot have *(a)* the circle's property of having all points on its perimeter being equidistant from some single point not on the perimeter and also have *(b)* the square's property of having all points on the perimeter not be equidistant from any single point not on the perimeter. These properties are mutually exclusive. And thus it is that there really is no coherent meaning behind the combination of concepts involved in "There is a geometric figure that simultaneously has the properties of a square and all and only the properties of a circle." But if there is no coherent meaning behind a logical contradiction, then a logically contradictory combination of concepts does not succeed in describing any state of affairs; thus, when it is said that even God cannot do what is logically contradictory, it is not conceded that there is anything that has been excluded from God's power. Inasmuch as a logically contradictory combination of concepts describes no thing, nothing has been excluded from the domain of God's omnipotence. Saint Thomas Aquinas[7] expressed this point by observing that "it is better to say that such things cannot be done, than that God cannot do them."[8] Better still, it seems to me, is to say that logical contradictions do not describe things at all; so in saying that God cannot do them, one is merely noting that they do not describe anything to be done. In evaluating whether the challenge posed by some proposed course of action has been met by one of God's doings, it must be possible to check whether God's doing matches the state of affairs proposed. But with a logical contradiction, there is no content to the challenge; thus, it is utterly meaningless to ask whether what was done rises to the challenge. And that is to say that a logically contradictory combination of concepts poses no challenge at all.

That God *created the universe ex nihilo* and not out of some preexisting matter is, of course, connected to the notion of omnipotence just sketched. First, it seems to be required by omnipotence in that a material realm that existed independently of God's creative power would not depend upon God for its existence and thus would seem to involve a limitation on God's power. That all things derive their existence from God is a logically consistent state of affairs; however, on the supposition that there is an existing material that did not derive its existence from God, it would follow that there is a logically possible state of affairs that God could not bring about. So omnipotence as defined above seems to demand creation ex nihilo. Fortunately, omnipotence also appears to license creation ex nihilo. As mysterious as it may be to consider something coming to be in a pure act of creation, it is not obviously contradictory; therefore, it would seem to be within the ambit of what omnipotence can do. Still, even though there is nothing obviously incoherent about the concept of creation ex nihilo, it is a notion that makes all the more difficult the task of formulating a satisfactory response to the problem of evil. Given that the very stuff of the universe was brought into existence by a pure act of creation, it is not open for the theist to contend that God did not prevent evil because He was limited by the matter at His disposal. There was no matter prior to God's making it; therefore, it can hardly be blamed for God's failure to have made a better universe.

Having thus clarified the conception of God that is the target of the problem of evil, we are also in a position to present the problem of evil in even sharper relief. Believing in a God that is all-good, all-knowing, all-powerful, and the ultimate source of all that exists leaves little room to accept the obvious fact that there is an abundance of evil in the world. A morally perfect being would prevent what evil it could prevent; a being that knows all would know of whatever means were available for preventing evil; and an infinitely powerful being would have all logically possible means at its disposal to do so. To further underscore the problem, it is important to note that all evils are what philosophers call contingent—their nonexistence can be supposed without contradiction. So it cannot be said that God lacks the means or the know-how or the motivation to prevent evil; yet there is an abundance of very bad things in the world. The choice, an atheist might contend, could not be clearer. Accept the obvious fact that there is evil and thus abandon belief in the omninatured God or cling to the omninatured God and thus embrace the willful ignorance involved in turning a blind eye to the horrors that confront us daily. Deciding whether these are the only options is the task of this book.

# EVIL
# BEYOND
# BELIEF

*Chapter One*

# The Logical Version
# of the Problem of Evil

It was late afternoon on August 15, 1949, in the Bitterroot Mountains of western Montana. Two young men raced toward the top of the northern ridge overlooking Mann Gulch. They were seventeen-year-old Robert Sallee and eighteen-year-old Walter Rumsey. Just below the crest of the ridge Rumsey collapsed in a juniper bush and was prepared to stay there, spent of energy and will to continue the climb. Sallee stopped too, looking down at his friend, waiting for Rumsey to get up before he would press on. Prodded by Sallee's gaze, Rumsey freed himself from the snarl of branches, and the two resumed their scrambling ascent. It was a simple gesture, Sallee's stopping for Rumsey. Under normal circumstances it would have been nothing more than an act of courtesy, a bit of fair play between young men, each measuring the other's endurance. But these were not normal circumstances and it was not each other they raced. "I guess I would be dead if he hadn't stopped," Rumsey would later recall. "Funny thing, though, he never said a word to me. He just stood there until I said it to myself, but I don't think he said anything. He made me say it." By pausing to wait for his friend, Sallee saved Rumsey's life. He also risked his own. On the heels of Rumsey and Sallee that day was a raging forest fire, the kind that smoke jumpers call a "blowup," the kind they fear most. The same fire claimed the lives of their fellow smoke jumpers and a park ranger who had hiked to the scene to lend a hand. Tragically, these others lost their lives precious seconds from escape. Seconds were precious that day, and the firefighters knew it. The heat searing their lungs as they fled up the face of the northern ridge of Mann Gulch made sure they knew it. Sallee knew, and yet he stopped to wait for Rumsey. He stopped to wait with a raging blowup mere seconds behind.[1]

Thirteen firefighters lost their lives in the Mann Gulch fire of 1949. A fourteenth would likely have joined them had it not been for one man's heroic pause. And it is in this, the heroism of Robert Sallee, that the story of the Mann Gulch tragedy intersects our discussion of the problem of evil. In reflecting on Robert Sallee's act we have occasion to wonder: If a human being is capable of risking so much to prevent evil, what possible excuse could God have for not doing the same?

Minutes after Sallee and Rumsey took refuge on a shale slope on the other side of the ridge and watched the fire pass mercifully around them, they heard a voice from above calling out. It was Bill Hellman. He hadn't been as lucky. He'd found no shale patch in which to take refuge. Rumsey and Sallee went to him and helped him to a flat boulder where he was able to stretch out; then Sallee took off down the mountain in search of help. Rumsey stayed with Hellman, and the two men prayed together silently. Though help finally came, Hellman's deliverance was short-lived. So severe were his burns that he died in a hospital in Helena the next day.[2] Rumsey and Sallee did all that they could to help their fellow smoke jumper. They likely cursed their inability to do more. Rumsey even prayed, turning for help to a being that could do more, but the only thing that happened was the inevitable natural consequence of being burned as severely as Hellman had been. Rumsey and Sallee pushed the limits of human endurance in their efforts to save Hellman, and for that we rightly praise them. This praise stands in stark contrast to what we are inclined to say of a being that had the power to intervene, knew what was at stake, was asked to intervene, and yet did nothing.

If an imperfect and vulnerable human being is capable of risking his very life to prevent evil, how can we possibly excuse a being without any vulnerabilities for not intervening? The answer, according to many philosophers, is that we cannot. That is why, they would continue, belief in God simply cannot be reconciled with the existence of any evil whatsoever. Given that God is all good, God would do whatever He could to prevent evil, for a good being—witness Robert Sallee—would prevent whatever evil it could prevent. Given that God is omnipotent and that evils are one and all contingent—their nonexistence can be supposed without contradiction—it follows that there is no evil that God could not prevent. Given that God is omniscient, it cannot be supposed that God failed to prevent some evil because he did not know about it or did not know how to prevent it. God's will is directly efficacious and God's vision is all-penetrating. All God would have to do is say the word, will that it be so, and any evil you want would have been prevented. And this means that if there were a God, there would be no evil. God's existence and the existence of evil simply cannot both be the case. Since we know that there is evil, we cannot escape the conclusion that there is no God. It would amount to a logical contradiction to say otherwise.

## The Logical Problem of Evil

The charge that it would amount to a contradiction to believe in both God and evil is sometimes referred to as the "logical" version of the problem of evil. The terminology seems to have originated with J.L. Mackie's essay "Evil and Omnipotence."[3] Unlike "evidentialist" versions of the problem that will be considered in later chapters, the logical version does not argue merely that the fact of evil renders God's existence highly unlikely; rather, the logical version contends that the fact of evil renders God's nonexistence an absolute certainty. In this respect the logical version poses the most serious challenge to theism of all versions of the problem of evil. Not only does it threaten those who claim that there is good reason to believe in God's existence or that the evidence for and against God's existence is pretty evenly balanced, it also threatens those theists who would maintain their belief through a pure act of faith. At the very least one must maintain that God's existence is possible if one is to believe in God on the basis of faith. But it is precisely the possibility of God's existence that the logical version of the problem targets, attempting to remove even the thread of a chance that there is a God. Attempting to say that one might have faith in God's existence while believing that God's existence is not possible would be rather like a scientist professing to have faith that time travel will some day be mastered even though he believed that it had been conclusively shown to be absolutely impossible.

Though in the respect just discussed the logical version of the problem poses the most serious challenge to theism, there are two respects in which it is the most vulnerable of versions of the problem of evil. The first is that it is much more difficult to prove that a conclusion is certainly true than it is to prove that it is likely true. That's one reason why our system of jurisprudence demands in criminal trials only that the accused be found guilty beyond a reasonable doubt. If it required that the accused be found guilty with logical certainty, few, if any, would ever be justly convicted. Consider the case of a man who stands accused of a double homicide. Imagine that there are several eyewitnesses to the crime; that the man's DNA was found all over the crime scene; that the victim's DNA was found all over the defendant's car, home, and clothing; and that he had confided in several acquaintances that he wanted to kill the individuals in question so as to receive a fifty-million-dollar inheritance. Now further imagine that virtually all of this evidence is unchallenged at trial. Yes, the defense concedes, it was the defendant's blood in all those places; and yes, he did stand to inherit a tidy sum; and yes, he did say the things he was alleged to have said; and yes, the eyewitnesses to the crime are sincere and credible. Having granted all this, however, they proceed to offer the following defense. There is a criminal genius known only as Manifold Specter, who is a master of disguise, of breaking and entering, and of forensic biology. It was Manifold Specter who actually did the crime while disguised to look like the accused. He also arranged to have all the DNA evidence planted in those places in which it was found. As for the defendant's rash comments to acquaintances, who among us has not been guilty of an ill-chosen word or two in a moment of pique? Now further imagine that the defense presents absolutely no evidence that these events happened, let alone that there is such a person. What they say to all requests to substantiate their version of the murders is that it is logically possible that there is such a person and it is logically possible that he did the deeds he is hypothesized to have done. That is, the defense maintains that their story is internally consistent as well as consistent with the evidence that has gone unchallenged. Now if our courts required that a defendant be shown guilty with absolute certainty such that the defendant's innocence could be upheld only under pain of contradiction, there is no doubt that our imaginary defendant should walk. Indeed, it is hard to imagine a trial that would not end in acquittal if the jurors were to be faithful to this absurdly high burden of proof. That it is extremely difficult to prove a conclusion with logical certainty is no less true of attempts to prove God's nonexistence than it is to prove other conclusions. All a theist need do is sketch a story that is internally consistent and that explains how evil might have entered the creation of a God who is all-knowing, all-powerful, and all-good.

The second respect in which the logical version of the problem of evil is vulnerable is that it does not appeal to specific kinds or instances of evil. It does not ask how belief in God can be reconciled with the appalling quantity of evil in the world. Nor does it ask how belief in God can be squared with certain cases of horrendous evil, like the savage abuse and murder of children. In its strict form, the logical version of the problem of evil sets aside all such specific considerations in alleging that God's existence cannot be reconciled with any evil whatsoever. The charge behind this strictest version of the problem is that if there is a God, there should be absolutely no evil whatsoever; therefore, if there is *any* evil in the world, it follows under pain of contradiction that God simply does not exist. And this means that the theist need only identify one instance of evil that would be consistent with the existence of God and the theist will have responded to the logical problem of evil.

Taking both of these points of vulnerability into account, it follows that a theist need only do the following to successfully respond to the logical version of the problem of evil: Select an evil of her choosing and then tell some logically consistent story of why God would allow this evil. It is important to remember that the theist need not give evidence for believing that the story is true, for as long as the story is internally coherent and does not violate any principle that is necessarily true, the theist will have met the threshold needed to rebut the logical version of the problem in its strictest form. The logical version of the problem of evil gives the apologist for theism the entire space of the logically possible in which to move.

Still, despite its vulnerability, the task of providing an adequate response to the logical version of the problem of evil is not a simple matter. Part of the reason is, of course, the theist's commitment to God's omnipotence. It is true enough, the advocate of the logical version of the problem of evil will say, that I have given the theist the entire space of the logically possible in which to fashion a reply. But the theist must not forget that God's alleged omnipotence gives God the entire space of the logically possible in which to combat evil. While it is easy to tell stories about good human beings who fail to prevent evil because they are unable, the prospects of telling a similar story about an omnipotent being do not look nearly as promising. Thus it is that the logical problem of evil is not quite so frail as it might first appear. Indeed, it will take me this chapter and four more to sketch what I take to be an acceptable answer to the challenge posed therein.

**The Free Will Defense**

The first point that many theists make in rebutting the logical version of the problem of evil is to note that the moral principle employed in the problem needs to be formulated with greater precision. It is simply not true, they will say, that a good being prevents any evil that it can prevent. Suffering is an evil, but good and loving parents will sometimes subject their children to medical treatment that involves suffering that is sometimes intense and prolonged. They subject their children to such treatment despite the suffering, because they are convinced that the treatment is their best chance of preserving a much greater good—the preservation of the child's health. The parents could, of course, prevent the pain involved in the treatment by simply not having their child treated. But this would be to forfeit a good—the child's future health—that is at least as great as the evil involved in the treatment. They opt therefore to treat and are thought right to do so. What cases like this make clear is that it is not quite right to say flatly that a good being will prevent whatever evil it can prevent. Really, the moral principle expressing the value of preventing evil must be closer to the following: A good being will prevent whatever evil it can prevent unless doing so would result in losing something at least as good.[4]

Now it may at first be unclear how this revision will help the theist. Unlike the parents who are limited in their options by the nature of the physical world, God labors under no such constraints. But if this needed revision of the moral principle behind the logical version of the problem of evil is to be of any help to the theist, the theist must identify some evil that God could not have prevented without thereby sacrificing something at least as good or permitting something at least as bad.

It will surely have occurred to many readers, including many who are not schooled in theology or philosophy, that there is an obvious candidate for an evil that God could not prevent without thereby forfeiting something at least as good or permitting something at least as bad. God gave human beings the great gift of freedom, it will be said, but genuine freedom includes the possibility that the freedom be used to do bad things. Thus it is that the inference from *any* evil in creation to an imperfection in the creator does not go through precisely because at least some of the evil in the universe is the direct result of free human choices. Now God was, of course, under no obligation to create free beings and thus could have prevented the existence of moral evil; however, it is far from clear that it would have been good for God to do this. It may well be the case that the universe is better by having free beings and moral evil than it would be if it lacked both moral evil and free beings. The good of free will is a good that enables us to love God and one another. It is a good that enables its possessor to chart her or his own destiny. It is a good that makes a possibility of the heroism of a Robert Sallee. It is a good that makes a possibility of the life of self-sacrifice of a Ghandi or a Martin Luther King Jr. It is a good that makes possible a husband's lifelong commitment to his wife and her's to him. For these and more reasons than there is space to mention, the good of free will is thus a good that may well justify God's bestowing it despite the unavoidable risk of its crueler manifestations.

This approach to the logical version of the problem of evil is known as the free will defense.[5] Though the logical version of the problem of evil is vulnerable, it is not quite so vulnerable as to wither immediately in the heat supplied by the free will defense, for there are a number of points at which the free will defense is itself vulnerable to attack. In particular, the conception of free action that stands behind the free will defense has been subjected to attack on two main fronts. First, it is sometimes alleged that contemporary science has shown **determinism** to be true and hence that there is no free will in the sense required by the free will defense. By "determinism" here I mean the view that at any moment in the history of the universe, the state of the universe at that time uniquely fixes all future events and states of affairs of the universe; that is, given the way things are at any given time, there is only one way that they can unfold in the future.[6] Insofar as such determinism is alleged to extend to all events without qualification, it equally extends to human choices and human actions and thereby shows that no human actions or choices are free.

I will spend very little time discussing this objection for the simple reason that there is no decisive evidence that science has shown us any such thing.[7] This is especially true of contemporary science where it is widely held that the behavior of subatomic particles does not conform to any straightforward deterministic model.[8] Moreover, even if science did paint an unequivocally deterministic picture of the universe, it is not clear that this would demand that free will be rejected. Whether it would entail the denial of free will would depend on what view one took of science. One respectable view of science is that it should be understood only as a kind of instrument used for making predictions about the natural world. The force of the "only" here is that on such an instrumental view of science it is deemed a mistake to view scientific theories as being in the business of giving an ultimate metaphysical account of what is, of telling us the way things really are. Such an understanding of science allows one to maintain that human choices really are free at the level of ultimate metaphysical reality even if science were to act as if the universe were a fully deterministic system.[9] And this is only to say that even if science were to ultimately embrace a deterministic model of the universe, arriving at the conclusion that there is no free will would depend upon settling some highly contentious issues about the nature of science itself. At any rate, given that science does not at present embrace a deterministic model of the universe, and given that even if it did we might still uphold the freedom of the will, I conclude that the natural sciences do not pose a special obstacle to advancing the thesis that human beings are free.

The second point at which the freedom of the free will defense is susceptible to attack, and one on which I will say a good deal more, is intimated by the first. The aforementioned but ill-fated contention that science shows determinism to be true and hence freedom impossible does rightly assume that the freedom that free will defenders allege to stand behind free human choices is a freedom that is incompatible with those same choices being causally determined. The thesis that it is inconsistent to believe both in a thoroughgoing determinism and in freedom is known as incompatibilism. Incompatibilists who are determinists and thus reject freedom are known as **hard determinists**. Incompatibilists who assert that there is freedom and thereby reject a thoroughgoing determinism, on the other hand, are known as voluntarists or **libertarians**.[10] Human actions are free for the libertarian only if they result from choices that are not themselves fully determined by any prior events or conditions. If this were not the case, and if an action's being free were compatible with its being causally necessitated, then it would certainly seem to be the case that God could have given human beings the gift of freedom and yet *caused* human beings to always choose the good. For the free will defense to get off the ground, the sense of freedom operative therein must be an incompatibilist sense that excludes the possibility that God has caused all human actions.

Now a reader unfamiliar with philosophical disputes about the nature of freedom is likely to greet this report with a shrug. At best it must seem like a rather obvious elaboration of the free will defense, but it hardly seems the starting point for an objection to it. It is, however, a point of no small significance. There is, you see, a long and rich history of extremely able philosophers who have held that human beings are free while at the same time insisting that this freedom is perfectly consistent with all human actions being causally determined. This theory of freedom is known as **compatibilism** or **soft determinism**. The challenge that it poses for the free will defense is that sketched at the end of the preceding paragraph; namely, if the compatibilist is right about the nature of freedom, then there is no reason that God couldn't have made human beings free and yet such that they never choose wrongly. Thus it is that the success of the free will defense hinges on showing that the libertarian account of freedom is superior to the compatibilist account. It hinges on being able to meet the compatibilist's challenge.

*Chapter Two*

# The Challenge of Compatibilism

"Compatibilism" is so called because it is the theory that freedom and determinism are compatible with one another. This is not simply the claim that it is possible for there to be free actions and causally determined actions that coexist within a single system in the way that one's free decision to swing a baseball bat can coexist with the physical forces that determine the ball's trajectory once it has left the bat. That there can be two different events where one of these events is a free action and the other is causally determined might be called the coexistence thesis and is a point that would be granted by all libertarians. The compatibility asserted by the compatibilist is far more dramatic a claim than that involved in the coexistence thesis. Compatibilism is the theory that one and the same action can be both free and causally determined by prior events. And the compatibilist is also not playing the game of saying that a free act is caused by one's choice but nonetheless free because the choice was not itself causally determined. The sense of determinism conceded by compatibilism is that which was defined in the preceding section. Compatibilism thus maintains that one's choice to freely perform some action was irretrievably in the cards at any past time you want to pick, including times long before one even existed.[1]

Stated so starkly, I am sure that some readers will find compatibilism highly counterintuitive and perhaps even suspect that it is nothing more than a perverse attempt by philosophers to display their cleverness by defending the patently absurd. While philosophy does suffer from its share of preciously perverse theories, compatibilism is not a case in point. To see that this is so and that the case that can be made for compatibilism is far from frivolous, a good beginning can be made by considering some examples of free and unfree action.

I am "blessed" with three older brothers. When we were growing up, they used to delight in grabbing my arm and swinging it so that my hand slammed repeatedly into my chest. I would try to stop them, of course, but I simply wasn't strong enough. So it was that they would slam my hand into my chest all the while asking in a tone of earnest concern, "What's wrong with you? Why do you keep hitting yourself? What's the matter with you!"[2] Needless to say, hitting myself in the chest was not an action that I was performing freely. This is clear from the fact that it was neither something that I wanted to do nor chose to do. It was, in this sense, against my will. Now contrast this case with one in which I would normally be thought to have acted of my own free will. On my way home from work I decide to give my family a special treat by stopping to pick up a bucket of livers from the Gobblin' Gizzard. I am, after all, a thoughtful spouse and always remember to do something extra special on my anniversary. Unlike the case of chest pounding, this was an action that was in keeping with what I wanted and what I chose to do; it was an action done of my own free will and not against it.

Now what the compatibilist wants you to notice about such contrasting cases is that in explaining the sense in which the first action was not free and the second one was, there was no need to insist that the choice behind the second action was itself an uncaused action. Indeed, the issue of whether the choice was itself causally determined never even arose. Whether the action was free or unfree was treated simply as a function of whether it resulted from a choice made by the individual in question. What this suggests is that the question of whether our choices are causally determined is irrelevant to the issue of whether our actions are free. But if it is irrelevant, then it makes no difference to the freedom of our actions whether they are fully causally determined or not, and this is to say that freedom and determinism are compatible.

This is not, of course, a full or adequate defense of compatibilism; nonetheless, it is enough to show that it is a challenge that the free will defender must take seriously. The reason that it is not an adequate defense of compatibilism on its own is that a libertarian will be quick to point out that it may well be that the absence of causally determining factors behind one's choices was not mentioned in the foregoing analysis of freedom and compulsion only because it was taken for granted. Perhaps we treat deciding whether an act is free as merely a matter of deciding whether it flowed from the actor's choice precisely because we naturally make the libertarian assumption that our choices themselves are not determined. That we regularly neglect this point in evaluating whether an act is free may only reflect our thinking that it goes without saying. Now even if this is the case, this is not grounds in itself for rejecting compatibilism. The libertarian's assumption may well be a precritical prejudice that it is best to cast aside in reaching a more accurate understanding of freedom and moral responsibility. It is, however, grounds for demanding that the compatibilist further develop his analysis of the difference between free and unfree actions. The libertarian contention that one's choices are uncaused provides an obvious difference between those actions that are chosen and hence free and those actions that are against one's will and hence unfree. Once we drop this assumption, as the compatibilist says we must, it is incumbent upon the compatibilist to explain why it matters that an act is chosen or wanted when its being chosen is as much a product of the causal machinery of the universe as are the motions of the planets about the sun. Saying that an act was done "freely" is to identify it as having a special significance. It is to say that it is a kind of action that stands apart from others—the unfree ones—in an important way. The challenge facing the compatibilist, then, is to offer some explanation of how a *causally necessitated* choice could possibly rise to the task of capturing the special significance that we accord an action when we identify it as one that is "free."

But how is the compatibilist to go about showing that his theory successfully captures the special significance that is accorded an action by calling it free? It will be of little help to the compatibilist to appeal to an intuition that freedom simply means "freedom to do as one chooses," for the libertarian will claim to have an equally strong intuition that freedom means "freedom from causal necessitation." What's needed is some way of getting a handle on the special significance of free action that does not assume either the compatibilist or the libertarian view of freedom. How this can be done becomes evident when we attend to the fact that we talk of human beings as having wills and as being capable of free action largely in order to express our conviction that a human being can be a source of action in a way that justifies our holding the human being responsible for the action. Why do we find it appropriate to describe a person's vandalizing another's property as reprehensible but do not even consider using this term to describe damage to a person's property that resulted from a flash flood? The quick answer is that a person has free will and the creek does not. Talk of wills and freedom thus often serves as shorthand for the fact that human beings are sources of action in a distinctive way, a way that justifies holding them morally accountable for the things that they do in this distinctive way. We talk of human beings as having free will to express the idea that a human being is an appropriate object of reward and punishment, praise and censure. This is not to say that our understanding of freedom has emerged entirely out of our conception of the nature of moral responsibility, for it may well be that our convictions concerning moral responsibility are ultimately derived from an independent awareness of the manner in which human action is distinctive and hence free. Nonetheless, it does not seem to me too strong to say that human freedom is so intimately connected to our willingness to hold human beings responsible that any successful theory of freedom must make sense of this willingness.[3] Thus it is that one can decide whether compatibilism is an acceptable theory of freedom by asking whether it makes sense of moral responsibility.

It was noted earlier that the compatibilist is faced with the challenge of explaining how a causally necessitated choice is able to ground the significance that we attach to an action by identifying it as a free action. When we attend to the intimate connection between freedom and moral responsibility, we can put this challenge as follows: If our wants and choices are as much causally necessitated as actions that are coerced or compelled, what possible difference between the two cases could there be that would justify holding an individual morally responsible in one case but not in the other? Why, in other words, should we make such a fuss, morally speaking, about chosen actions once it has been conceded that choices are no more exempt from causal determinism than other parts of the natural order? It is a question with a formidable ring and thus considerable rhetorical force. It's also a question that the compatibilist is eager to answer. When one moves beyond treating it as a merely rhetorical question and actually attempts to answer it, says the compatibilist, one sees two things. First, that compatibilism can make sense of moral responsibility. Second, that the alternative, libertarianism, is an utter failure in this respect.

## Compatibilism and Personal Responsibility

Imagine that the duty of eulogizing a friend has fallen to you. What sorts of things would you say?

> Jack Rascal was born in 1961, grew to a height of six feet two and had a weight that fluctuated between 200 and 250 pounds. His eyes were green and his hair brown. He had two bouts with pneumonia, the first one occurring ten years before the one that caused his death. In 1983 he had a wart removed from his left index finger. The method of removal was freezing. He owned numerous toothbrushes until his thirty-first birthday. It was then that he received a Waterpik as a birthday present. He was right-handed and never played pinball, though he did play fussball three times. His Social Security number was . . .

Whatever you would say, it most surely would not be this. What's wrong with it as a eulogy, in part, is that it does nothing to convey who the *person* Jack Rascal was. It tells us nothing about his hopes ("He dreamed of being a tenor for the Boston Pops"), his wants ("What he wanted more than anything else was for his children to have more opportunities than he'd had"), his character ("If he told you he'd help you move your stuff, he'd be the first one to show up and the last to leave"), his sense of humor ("Can any who were close to him ever again hear the phrase 'Whoa, who floated the trial balloon?' without thinking of Jack?"), his tastes ("I guess the Gobblin' Gizzard's going to be closing its doors now"), his passions ("While he gave of his time and money to all who needed, his heart belonged only to Janet 'Jacksie' Rascal").

Now what all of this has to do with compatibilism is that many of the same factors that we take to be central to defining who a person is are the very same factors that a compatibilist will say causally determine the person's choices. We make the choices that we do, the compatibilist would say, because we have the beliefs, desires, passions, and character traits that we do. The difference between a free and unfree act thus has nothing to do with one being caused and the other not. What it has to do with is that the free act is caused by factors that are central to defining who the actor is whereas the unfree act is caused by factors that really have nothing to do with the actor as a person. That my brothers enjoyed the game of slamming my fist into my chest is a fact about them, not about me. On the other hand, the choice that caused me to drive through the Gobblin' Gizzard was itself caused by factors that are part of the story of who I am as a person; that is, it was caused by my beliefs, desires, emotions, and character traits. In this way, a compatibilist will allege that actions that flow from one's choices bear a significant connection to who one is as a person, in that such chosen actions are ultimately caused by factors that are central to one's being the person that one is. And given that chosen actions are thus intimately connected to the person that performs them, it makes sense to hold the person morally accountable for such actions.

Compatibilists will thus point out that their theory of freedom is true to our conviction that the actions one chooses to perform are actions that reflect the kind of person one is. Virtuous deeds reflect a person of virtuous character—a person whose beliefs, desires, emotions, and habits all conspire to cause charitable choices on the whole. Vicious deeds reflect a person of vicious character—a person whose beliefs, desires, emotions, and habits all conspire to cause vicious choices on the whole. Since choices are caused by and thus indicative of the character of the person who made them, it makes sense to take those choices to redound to the quality of the person who made them. Thus it is that we have a basis for praising the person who does the virtuous deed and censuring the person who does the vicious deed, even though both deeds are causally determined.

The thrust of this argument in defense of compatibilism can be summarized by saying that compatibilism is very good at satisfying what I will call the **Ownership Condition** for moral responsibility. The idea behind the Ownership Condition is that a person should be held responsible for an action only if the person is the causal source of the action.[4] The Ownership Condition is satisfied by compatibilism, its advocates would say, because it identifies the cause of one's actions as one's choices, and then identifies the causes of one's choices as psychological facts that are constitutive of the person one is.

Now some readers, I'm sure, will think the Ownership Condition to be an obvious requirement for moral responsibility. Indeed, it may seem too obvious to even be worth mentioning; too obvious to make compatibilism's satisfying it much cause for the compatibilist to celebrate. But the significance of the Ownership Condition, the compatibilist can retort, is more to be found in its breach than in its observance. For while compatibilism can make a strong case for satisfying this condition, there is good reason to think that libertarianism fails to come close to satisfying this most obvious requirement for moral responsibility. The basic problem, as the compatibilist sees it, is that libertarianism does not provide any basis for concluding that the action is something done by the person. The libertarian does say that the action is prompted by a choice made by the person; but this establishes a tenuous connection at best, for there is no causal connection between the choice and anything else about the person. The libertarian, remember, insists that a truly free choice is not causally determined by any prior states or events of the agent. It is not, for instance, causally necessitated by the agent's beliefs, desires, emotions, or character traits. But if there is nothing about the person that causally determines what choice is made, then it is not clear why we should think of the choice as something done by the person. Since there is nothing about the person that causally ushers in the choice, there is no more reason to think of the choice as something that the person does than there is to think of the choice as something that happens to the person. And if there is no good reason to think of the choice as something that the person does, then there is no good reason to think of the action prompted by the choice as something that the person does either. And if there is no good reason to think of a chosen action as something that the person does, then there is no good reason to hold the person accountable for the action. Libertarianism would thus seem to make of a chosen action a sort of behavioral tic of the human being. Is it not, the compatibilist will ask, far more sensible to view a chosen action as a causal manifestation of the person that the human being is? Does this not make far more sense of our willingness to hold people responsible for their actions? Thus it is that the Ownership Condition poses no small challenge to libertarianism. Indeed, many compatibilists take it to be decisive.[5]

But the success of compatibilism and the alleged failure of libertarianism in handling the Ownership Condition are not yet enough to make compatibilism the theory of choice in making sense of moral responsibility, for there is more to moral responsibility than the concerns captured by the notion of act ownership. As we shall see in the remainder of this chapter, what more there is casts serious doubt on the claim that compatibilist theories of freedom can make sense of moral responsibility.

## Compatibilism and the Avoidability Condition

Consider how appalling we would find it for a father to berate his seven-year-old son for being unusually small for his age. "Why do you have to be so puny?" he asks in disgust when he learns that his son's lunch money has been stolen for the third time that week. "Some kindergartners are bigger than you. Maybe I should hire one of them to be your bodyguard. Yeah, that's what I'll do. I'll hire Rebecca Rascal. She's just graduated from preschool. She can protect your pathetic hide." We would find such behavior appalling for the stunningly shallow values that motivate it. But we would find it no less appalling for the fact that his size is not a thing that a seven-year-old boy has any control over. It is not something that he could have avoided by acting differently, and it is, therefore, not something for which the child should be chastised. This latter reason that we would be aghast at the father's behavior is an illustration of a second general condition for moral responsibility that might be called the **Avoidability Condition**.[6] The idea behind the Avoidability Condition for moral responsibility is that a person should be praised or blamed and rewarded or punished for an action only if the person could have avoided or prevented the action or state of affairs for which he is being held accountable.[7] They should be held accountable for the way things are, that is, only if they could have made them other than they are. The relevance of this condition to present concerns is that it is frequently alleged by libertarians and hard determinists that compatibilism fails to satisfy this crucial condition of moral responsibility. It fails to satisfy this condition insofar as compatibilism maintains that all human actions are fully causally necessitated and thus are, strictly speaking, no more preventable *by us* than the orbit of Io about Jupiter or the inability of blue whales and wombats to mate or the date of one's birth or the natural color of one's eyes. Actions that flow from a person's wants *seem* to be more within one's control, but this seeming is readily recognized as an illusion when the determinism inherent in compatibilism is carried to its logical conclusion. If determinism is true, then all of our psychological states are the result of causal chains that can be traced back to factors and causes that existed even before we were born, and thus back to factors that we are and have always been powerless to prevent.[8]

As initially plausible as this argument is, many compatibilists are largely unmoved by it. They are unmoved because they believe that the alleged inability of compatibilism to satsify the Avoidability Condition is really based on a misunderstanding of the true nature of the Avoidability Condition of moral responsibility. What moral responsibility requires, it is said, is not that it really was possible for the agent to have done otherwise; rather, the requirement is only that the agent would have done otherwise *if he had chosen to do otherwise*. This view, which we can call the Conditional Analysis of Avoidability, interprets the requirement that the agent "could have done otherwise" as having an implicit condition upon it, the condition that the agent chose otherwise. Thus it is, our compatibilist would say, that the ability to do otherwise required for moral responsibility is a conditional and not an absolute ability. On such a Conditional Analysis, the Avoidability requirement should be rewritten as follows: A person should be held morally responsible for an action only if he could have done otherwise if he had chosen to do otherwise.[9]

What rewriting the avoidability requirement does for compatibilism is enable it to make sense of a person's having been able to do otherwise even when what the person did was itself fully determined. Consider your choice to get the bucket of livers at the Gobblin' Gizzard. According to a compatibilist, it was an action that had to happen, for it was as much a causally determined action as any other event within nature. Nonetheless, the proximate cause of the action was the agent's choice to perform the action; therefore, it can truly be said that if you had not chosen to buy a bucket of livers, then you would not have done so.

What this analysis of avoidability has going for it is that it ties in with our intuition that an action for which an individual should be held accountable is an action that turns upon the choice that the individual made. If an agent's having chosen otherwise is sufficient for his having acted otherwise, then his action is free and one for which he should be held morally accountable. This is to be contrasted with cases in which it didn't matter what the person chose, for the presence or absence of the person's choice had no bearing on the outcome. Consider the following scenario.

Two students fail to show up for the same final exam. The first student stopped by a bank on the way to school, only to be locked into the bank vault by a group of bank robbers. The other student missed the exam because it was a beautiful day and he decided he'd rather go to the beach instead of spending the day in a stuffy classroom answering questions about the Riemann-Stieltjes integral and Fourier series. The first student, of course, should not be held responsible for her failure to take the exam, because her failure to do so was not something that she chose. It is, consequently, not something that could have been changed if only she had chosen to take the test. She could choose all she wanted while locked in that vault. Her choices would have gotten her nowhere. The beach boy, on the other hand, will not be allowed to take a makeup exam, will fail the course, and, really, deserves no sympathy. His predicament was of his own choosing. In his case, had he simply chosen to come to class, he could have avoided the whole mess.

Now what the compatibilist would want us to notice about this scenario is how natural it is to make the efficacy of choice the central concern in deciding whether the person is to be held responsible for what transpired. The compatibilist would also want us to take special note of the last sentence of the above scenario, a sentence that reveals how natural it is to connect avoidability with the person's having chosen otherwise: "Had he simply *chosen* to come to class, he could have *avoided* the whole mess." It would thus be unfair to suggest that the Conditional Analysis of Avoidability is simply an ad hoc addendum that compatibilists have tacked on to the avoidability requirement just to get out of a problem. It is a reading of the Avoidability Condition that resonates with the manner in which we make ascriptions of responsibility. This is not to say, however, that the centrality of choice to the ascription of moral responsibility gives anything like conclusive evidence for the Conditional Analysis interpretation of avoidability. Indeed, a libertarian also will emphasize the importance of choice to the issue of accountability. Even more important, however, is the fact that there is a morally significant sense of avoidability that is not covered by the Conditional Analysis of Avoidability. In the next section, I turn to the task of showing that this is so.

## Avoiding Ourselves

In thinking of the avoidability of an action, it is appropriate to ask not merely whether a different choice by the agent would have resulted in a different outcome but also whether the agent could have made a different choice. It is well and good to say that an agent is responsible if he would have done otherwise if he had so chosen; however, it is surely relevant to ask whether the agent could have so chosen. Consider a person who has been hypnotized so that whenever he hears Christmas carolers at his door, he is programmed to choose to pour water on the carolers from a second-floor window. Given that the man was making hypnotically induced choices, we would surely not want to hold the man responsible for dousing the carolers. Moreover, the reason we would give for not holding the man responsible is that he was unable to avoid doing what he did, given the way he'd been hypnotized. Nonetheless, it is true of this man that he would have refrained from dousing the carolers if he had chosen to do so. His problem and the reason he was not responsible is that he could not have chosen to refrain. This suggests that avoidability requires more than a mere ability to have done otherwise if one had chosen to do so. It would also seem to require the ability to have made a different choice than one did.

There are, it seems to me, two distinct though closely related strategies that a compatibilist might try at this point. First, she might concede that a person's having been able to choose otherwise is a requirement for moral responsibility and then proceed to give a conditional analysis of this ability so that the phrase "could have chosen otherwise" is understood to mean "would have chosen otherwise if he had wanted to." Of course, one might then wonder whether the individual could have wanted otherwise. If we imagine that the hypnotist has acted upon his subject in such a way that, whenever he hears carolers, he has a desire to douse and it is this desire that causes him to choose to do the deed, we are really no closer to having an act that we think the individual should be held responsible for. Now a compatibilist might try to handle this problem by giving a conditional analysis of being able to desire otherwise, where the ability to desire otherwise is conditional upon having still other mental states in place. The compatibilist might say, for instance, that "could have desired otherwise" really means "would have desired otherwise, if he had felt or reasoned otherwise." But this is only to delay the inevitable, for the same question will again be asked about deliberation or emotion or whatever mental event is selected. For example, one might ask whether the person could have avoided the deliberation that caused the desire that caused the choice that caused the action. The problem, of course, is that if the compatibilist continues to acquiesce to the voluntarist's demand that each psychological condition along the way must itself be avoidable, the compatibilist will soon reach conditions that have nothing to do with the individual. Given his commitment to determinism, once the compatibilist traces the causal conditions back far enough, he will reach events and states of affairs that existed before the individual even existed, causal conditions that "might have been otherwise" but not as a result of anything having to do with the agent in question.

For this reason, the compatibilist will have to stop this series of questions before it starts to cause trouble. The compatibilist will have to point to one of the questions in the series and say that its demand for avoidability is out of place. Where the compatibilist will make his stand will depend, of course, on which version of compatibilism one is dealing with. Nonetheless, a stand he must make, and the general form of the stand will be something like the following.

You were right to say that the man who chooses to douse the carolers as a result of hypnotic suggestion would not be accountable for his action; however, you have incorrectly explained why he is not accountable. It is not because his choice was not avoidable. It was, rather, because his choice did not flow from psychological factors that define who he is as a person. The choice that he made did not flow from his desires, his emotions, his character traits, or his deliberations. It did not flow from him. What it flowed from was something that the hypnotist did to him. And the same could be said for other forms of mind control, such as the use of chemicals or brainwashing. Indeed, when it comes to actions performed under the influence of mind-altering drugs, we already have idioms that reflect our belief that there is a sense in which it

is not really the person who is acting. An acquaintance propositions your wife at a party, but the next day your friends reassure
you that he didn't mean it. "He's not like that" they say. "That
wasn't him talking. That was just the beer." And the metaphor of
brain "washing" is also instructive here, for the suggestion is that
the victim's personality has been washed away and replaced with
a different, alien one. That the victim of brainwashing is not responsible for what he's choosing is not because he has been caused
to act as he does; rather, it is because "he" has been washed away
and thus is not really the one doing the acting. It would, of course,
be silly to read too much into such figures of speech; nonetheless,
they do illustrate the compatibilist's basic point here. What is required for one to be responsible for one's choices is that the choices
flow from those psychological traits that define the person that
one is. It is in no way necessary to think that the person could have
chosen otherwise.[10] This, of course, amounts to making ownership the dominant condition in assigning moral responsibility. In
essence, what the compatibilist is saying is that the need to satisfy
the Avoidability Condition ends at the point when it is clear that
the Ownership Condition has been satisfied; that is, when the action is seen to be caused by psychological traits that are essential
to the person in question.

But this is not a very satisfying response. For one thing, if the
compatibilist rides the Ownership Condition so hard, she will wind
up having to concede that any actions that are contrary to an
individual's character are actions for which the individual is not
responsible. Any occasion, that is, on which an individual makes a
choice that is not in keeping with her more enduring character,
would have to be an occasion on which she is not fully responsible
for her action. Second, and perhaps more important, it is not at all
clear that the need for avoidability ends where ownership begins.
The reason that it is not at all clear is that it would appear, prima
facie, to be a legitimate question bearing on moral responsibility
to ask whether an individual could have avoided becoming the
person that she has become. Could she have avoided herself? And
if the answer comes back—as it must for the compatibilist—"No,

she couldn't have avoided herself," then it is not at all clear that the individual should be held accountable for her actions. This, it seems to me, is precisely why defense attorneys will sometimes document the savage abuse that a client experienced in his youth. The suggestion is that the monster that the individual has become is something that he had either no control or limited control over. It was the abuse he suffered at the hands of his parents that made him the coldhearted killer sitting before you. He never chose to become this person. Now I can certainly see why many would greet such defenses with a good measure of incredulity. Indeed, I find them rather dubious myself. Nonetheless, the reason for my skepticism is that I am not convinced that the abused do not have it within themselves to transcend their upbringings. That is to say, I do not see good reason for concluding that a person who was subjected to abuse does not therefore have significant control over the person he or she becomes. If, however, it could be shown conclusively that a person really had no control over who he became and that who he is completely determines what he will do on all occasions, then I, for one, would be loathe to conclude that he is morally responsible.[11]

Now a compatibilist might be tempted to respond to this objection by saying that it is simply false to conclude that compatibilism does not leave room for an individual to avoid becoming the person that he or she became. A person could have avoided becoming the person that she did by making different choices along the way. After all, a large part of the characters that we become is a function of the actions that we perform. Granted, the individual could have no more made different choices along the way than she could have chosen to be born a week earlier; nonetheless, the fact remains that the individual would have been a different person had she made different choices. And this means that she does have control—albeit in a conditional sense—over the person that she became.

At this point, however, the compatibilist's position collapses into circularity. We cannot make the hallmark of a culpable choice the fact that it was caused by the person's character and then turn around and make the moral significance of the person's character dependent upon whether it resulted from the person's choices. If those choices are ones that flow from the person's already formed character, then the question of avoiding oneself has only been pushed back a step, for it can then be asked about the character behind those character-forming choices. If, on the other hand, the choice does not flow from the person's character—perhaps because there is no character yet in place—then it follows that the person is not responsible for being the person he has become insofar as the choices that forged this personhood are not choices that have the essential characteristic of a culpable choice.

A more promising compatibilist response would be to suggest that the objection is based on a misconstrual of the nature of moral accountability. When we say that people are accountable for their actions, the compatibilist might say, all we are saying is that it is appropriate to reward and punish them. Moreover, that this is appropriate means only that rewards and punishments can be expected to either reinforce or reform the individual's character. Thus it is that moral accountability does not require that the individual have control over who he has become, for to hold a person accountable is simply to observe that their character needs to be reinforced or reformed and to take appropriate steps to bring this about.[12]

If it is true that reinforcement and reformation are all that there is to rewarding and punishing, then it is clear that we need not worry about how an individual came to be the person that he is when we decide how to mete out rewards and punishments. All we need worry about is whether he is the kind of person whose character we want to encourage or the kind we want to discourage. But it is hard not to feel that something has been lost by reducing accountability to reinforcement and reformation. It feels like an evisceration of our ordinary understanding of moral accountability. It is, of course, one thing to feel that something has been lost and quite another to show it. If I don't get to watch my favorite football team on television and they lose, I feel—quite irrationally, of course—that they might have won had I been able to watch the game. Perhaps it is likewise illusory to feel that something important is missing in this account of accountability. In the next section, I argue that our sense of loss in this case is not an illusion at all.

## Between Retribution and Reform

What the reduction of accountability to reinforcement and reformation leaves out is the notion that punishment and reward are retribution for an individual's behavior. Rewards and punishments are not, that is, merely directed to strengthening or altering an individual's character. They are, rather, directed to giving an individual what he or she deserves. That this is part of our normal understanding of accountability becomes evident when we think about what form punishment and reward might take in a compatibilist future. Here we might consider the fate of two men. One has stolen some stereo equipment from the warehouse at which he works. The other is guilty of a savage murder. What it will take in our imagined future to reform the characters of these two criminals is the same—a pill. The chemical composition of the pill will be different in both cases, but it is a pill and a pill alone that will be needed to ensure that both will refrain from doing the same kind of thing in the future. On compatibilist assumptions about the nature of accountability and punishment, there would be nothing whatsoever inappropriate about punishing these men only by administering the medication. That, on a compatibilist story about punishment, would be precisely the thing to do.

But notice how distant that seems from our normal understanding of accountability. Our understanding of accountability demands that a person get what he deserves and that the punishment must be as proportional to the crime as it can be. That all that happens to these individuals is that each must take a pill strikes us as an abomination. It seems similarly outrageous that the murderer receives no harsher a penalty than the thief. Justice, we would be inclined to say, has not been done, for neither of these individuals received their due.

The compatibilist, however, would press on undeterred. What

you call retribution, he would say, is really just an institutional-
ized form of the primitive urge for revenge. This is not to say that
our primitive urge for revenge has been bad. Indeed, it may well
have been the most effective tool of character development and
deterrence at our disposal. But if we were to reach the point where
character could be reliably transformed medicinally, the need for
this primitive tool would have been replaced with a more precise
and effective tool. And surely we would be acting in a barbarous
manner if we did not replace the cruel and imprecise practice of
retribution—a practice that feeds the more savage of our inclinations—with the precise, effective, and humane practice of medicinally inducing reformation.[13]

Now the crucial moves in the compatibilist's response here are
the identification of retribution with revenge and the identification of revenge with deterrence. But there is good reason to be
suspicious of these moves. To see why, we need only reflect on the
fact that there can be acts of revenge and deterrence that do not
satisfy the requirement of desert. It might be an effective deterrent
(or revenge, for that matter) to kill the child of a child killer, but
such revenge would be unjust because of the obvious fact that the
child of the killer does not deserve to be killed.

Thus it is that compatibilism can go only so far in making sense
of holding human beings morally accountable for their actions.
The extent to which it is successful in this enterprise depends on
the extent to which we are willing to accept the compatibilist's
reinterpretation of some of our fundamental convictions of moral
responsibility. In particular, it depends upon whether we are willing to abandon the concept of desert as a legitimate concern in the
determination of moral responsibility. That last, it seems to me, is
a fairly drastic move in that it violates one of our most fundamental intuitions about the nature of accountability. Perhaps such a
drastic revision is in order. Indeed, a compatibilist might claim
that it is part of a philosopher's job to scrutinize our precritical
intuitions and concepts and bring to them a greater clarity, precision, and coherence. If doing so in the case of moral responsibility
demands rewriting the Avoidability Condition and abandoning our

commitments to desert, then so be it. And to find incentive to undertake these revisions, the compatibilist could continue, we need only recall that the alternative is incoherence. We must not forget the problem that the libertarian has with satisfying the Ownership Condition. Whereas compatibilism may force us to revise our conception of accountability, libertarianism encourages us to hold a person responsible for an action that cannot meaningfully be traced to him or her. While the compatibilist's position may cause some cognitive discomfort, the libertarian position commits us to the absurd. It encourages us to hold people responsible for actions that we cannot even say they did.

This last argument, it seems to me, is particularly instructive, for it emphasizes what may well be the decisive reason that many philosophers are compatibilists; that is, they believe that the alternative, libertarianism, makes no sense. Given the choice between the revision of our understanding of moral responsibility and a theory that is ultimately incoherent, says the compatibilist, we must surely choose the path of revision.

Faced with those alternatives, it is hard to quarrel with the compatibilist's choice. But is the alternative to compatibilism really incoherence? In the next chapter I argue that it is not so.

# Chapter Three

# A Case for Libertarianism

The crux of the free will defense as outlined in the preceding chapter is that it may well be the case that God could not have prevented all moral evil without forfeiting a most valuable aspect of creation; namely, beings who act freely. But it was there conceded that this defense makes sense only if freedom is understood in libertarian terms. If freedom were consistent with causal necessitation, as the compatibilist contends, there would seem to be no obstacle to an omnipotent God creating free beings such that they were caused to always do what is morally correct. A compatibilist theory of freedom would allow God to prevent all moral evil without compromising freedom a whit. No, it must be a libertarian freedom upon which rests the free will defense. And given where we left the libertarian at the end of the preceding chapter, perhaps it ought to be said that it is a libertarian freedom upon which teeters the free will defense. Such is the prima facie force of the ownership objection against libertarianism. It is an objection that calls into question not merely the truth of libertarianism, but also its very coherence. And given that the very coherence of libertarianism is put in question, so too is the success of the free will defense as a solution to the logical problem of evil. In the preceding chapter much was made of the fact that the threshold for a successful response to the logical version of the problem of evil is low; nonetheless, it is not so low as to forgive a central incoherence in the theist's story. Thus it is that the free will defender must exonerate the free will defense from this charge of incoherence. If she cannot do so, she must give up singing the praises of libertarian freedom; for what is nonsense can lay no claim to nobility. She must explain how it can make sense to hold persons responsible for libertarian free actions. She must explain how it makes sense to hold a person responsible for choices that were caused by no other event or state of the person who makes the choice. Only if libertarianism can withstand the charge of incoherence will the free will defense succeed. A first step in establishing its coherence is that of responding to the Ownership Objection.

## Ownership and Agent Causality

What was meant by the Ownership Objection in the preceding chapter is the charge that it would not make sense to hold a person accountable for a libertarian action because there is no basis by which a person's ownership of such an action might be established. By definition, a libertarian free choice is not caused by some prior states of the person in question; therefore, there is nothing about the person to which one can anchor the choice. If there is nothing that happens in the person to cause the choice, what sense is there in saying that it is the person who made the choice? We may as well say that the choice is something that happened to the person as that it is something that the person did. But if this is true, then a libertarian choice and the action that follow in its wake fail to satisfy the Ownership Condition of moral responsibility.

One way to respond to this objection has been to note that it rests upon the assumption that all causality is event causality. It depends, that is to say, on the view that the only kind of causality there is is that which is found in one event's being caused by another. Event causality is what we normally think of when we think of causal connections. An instance of lightning is the cause of an instance of thunder, the striking of one billiard ball by another is the cause of the first billiard ball's movement, my drinking of castor oil is the cause of my throwing up, Gilligan's boiling of coconuts in their shells is the cause of their exploding. . . . You get the idea: Event causality is the kind of causality in which one happening brings about another happening.

That the Ownership Objection assumes that all causality is event causality suggests a way out for the libertarian. It leaves open the possibility that there are kinds of causality other than event causality, other kinds of causality that might establish an agent's ownership of a libertarian free choice. In fact, this is precisely what some libertarians have maintained, claiming that the kind of causality behind libertarian choices is **agent causality.** The idea behind the term is that it is the agent or person—and not some event within the agent—that is the source of the action. In answer to the question of what caused a libertarian free choice, the advocate of agent causality would simply say "the person" and further refuse to specify some event or state within the person that causally determined that particular choice. The person just does it, and that's the end of the causal history of the choice. Cases of agent causality are cases in which a particular substance initiates a brand new causal pathway by causing an event—in this case a choice—that itself was not caused by any prior event. Thus it is that the advocate of agent causality offers the following response to the Ownership Objection: the agent owns a libertarian free choice because it is the agent who did it. Furthermore, the libertarian might continue, agent causality establishes the ownership of an action in a richer sense than does event causality. On agent causality, it is not some event or set of events within the agent that causes the action; rather, it is the agent qua substance that causes the action. In the case of event causality, one might say that it is the events within the agent and not the agent proper that have ownership of the action, whereas in agent causality it is the agent proper that has ownership of the action.

Now if the notion of agent causality makes sense, it could go a long way toward showing that libertarian freedom is coherent, for it could be used to answer those who maintain that there is no causal connection between the agent and a libertarian free choice. Indeed, if it does make sense to believe that a person qua substance is the cause of the free choice, then it would likewise make sense to believe that the person causally "owns" the choice even though there are no other prior events within the person which causally necessitate the choice. These, however, are rather substantial ifs, for the concept of agent causality has been received in philosophical circles with about as much enthusiasm as a tanning bed salesman at a vampire convention.[1]

What many philosophers find puzzling about agent causality is that a case of agent causality is not a case in which the agent undergoes some change and therefore is caused to act in a certain way, for this would simply be another instance of event causality. To be a distinctive kind of causality, agent causality must involve the agent initiating some action where the event of the agent's doing so is not caused by any preceding event, even one within the agent. And when agent causality is put thus, another problem emerges, a problem that seems to call into question the very point agent causality was intended to establish, namely, the person's ownership of libertarian free action. Given that there are no preceding events within the agent that cause the agent to choose as he or she does, it looks as if there is no basis from which to say that it is the person that actually causes the alleged free event.

To see this, we might conduct a thought experiment that would seem at first glance to be far removed from the issue of free action. Imagine that you have in your possession a shiny black rock. Further suppose that at uneven intervals and for varying durations, this rock has a bright red hourglass shape appear on its surface. You call it the Black Widow's Stone. Puzzled by this feature of your rock, you take it to scientists who begin to study it to determine what it is that causes the rock to develop this dramatic mark from time to time. After much study, the scientists conclude that the hourglass appears even when there are no events either within or without the stone that could possibly have caused the phenomenon, for it has appeared even when nothing else is happening in the stone or the stone's environment. The appearance of the hourglass, the scientists conclude, is not an instance of event causality, for there are no plausible candidates for events that might serve this role. And it is at this point that the Black Widow's Stone engages our discussion of agent causality. For the question now becomes: Should we conclude that the appearance of the hourglass is something that the stone does? Would it not be truer to think of the hourglass as something that happens on the stone without specifying that it is caused by the stone?

The point of the story, of course, is that persons as agents are in precisely the same situation as the stone. From time to time we make choices; however, there are no events within us that cause the choices that we make. So why should we believe that the choices are something we do as opposed to something that merely happens within us? And if we have no reason for supposing such events to be caused by ourselves, as opposed to happening to us, then the very thing that agent causality was introduced to establish—ownership of libertarian free actions—has not been established at all.

Now as with all thought experiments, this one has its limits. For there is something that persons can do that the Black Widow's Stone cannot. Persons can communicate. And one of the things that many persons report is an awareness or experience of the fact that they themselves are the source of their choices. That it is they as conscious beings who are behind their choices is reflected by the fact that they experience themselves as acting with an end in view, where such acting is acting with an awareness of what one is doing and an awareness of the end that one pursues in doing it. So, unlike the case of the rock, there is in human beings some basis for attributing the occurrence of a choice to the person as agent. This is not to say that this proves that human beings are free in a libertarian sense. It is to say, however, that barring further evidence to the contrary—such as an account that would explain away what human beings experience—we should do what we do in other cases of fairly widespread human experience. We should trust it.[2] And in trusting it, we are in position to see that libertarian choice is not quite as incoherent as the Ownership Objection would make it out to be. It is not quite so incoherent for the simple reason that agent causality puts the libertarian in position to argue that there is a causal connection between a free choice and the person who makes this choice.

Still, it is important not to overstate the victory that agent causality has won for the compatibilist at this point, for all that has been conceded thus far is that agent causality is a viable causal notion that we have some reason to believe is at work in human action. What has not been shown, however, is that agent causality establishes ownership of actions in a way that is morally meaningful, in a way that grounds moral responsibility and ascriptions of praise and blame. Indeed, in the course of attacking compatibilism in the preceding chapter, much was made of the fact that the kind of causal genesis of actions advocated by compatibilism was inconsistent with moral responsibility. Yes, of all philosophers, a libertarian should be perhaps most keenly aware of the fact that a coherent account of freedom must do more than merely establish a person's causal ownership of his actions. In appealing to agent causality to respond to the Ownership Objection, a libertarian must be sensitive to the issue of whether the kind of causal ownership established is contrary to the assignment of moral responsibility. And when this issue is considered, it becomes readily apparent that there is a serious reason to doubt that the kind of causal ownership persons can have of their libertarian choices—via an account of agent causality—is a causal ownership that is not consistent with holding persons accountable for the actions that they freely choose to perform.

## Libertarian Freedom and the Chance Objection

A libertarian free choice, it must be remembered, is a choice that is not causally determined by any prior events or states within the agent. Suppose the agent to have whatever beliefs, desires, reasons, and character traits you wish in the moment preceding choice, such factors do not causally determine that a certain choice will be made according to the libertarian. As we saw in the preceding section, this need not mean that the choice is uncaused or not caused by the person, for the possibility of agent causality enables one to say that it may be the person—and not any event or state or set of events or states within the person—that is the causal source of the choice. Nonetheless, it might be taken to imply that the agent is not the cause of the action in a morally significant way. That the person qua substance is the cause of the choice is all well and good, the opponent of libertarianism might observe, but the fact that the causality at work does not follow any causal laws seems to make the person's production of a libertarian choice a rather random affair. Given its insistence that there are no psychological events or factors that causally determine a libertarian free choice, libertarianism would seem to make of the agent a kind of random choice generator. And whatever we are willing to hold a person responsible for doing, we surely do not want to hold a person responsible for an outcome that happens at random or by chance. That is, however, precisely what we would be doing were we to hold people responsible for their libertarian choices. In the end, there is simply no way to distinguish between a libertarian choice and a chance event; therefore, a willingness to hold a person responsible for the former entails a willingness to hold them responsible for the latter. And since we certainly don't want to do that, we shouldn't hold them responsible for the former. And this means that libertarianism is a failure in the one crucial test that any theory of freedom must pass: It does not make sense of our ascriptions of moral responsibility.[3] According to this objection, the most that agent causality can do is establish an agent's bare causal ownership of an action. What it cannot do, however, is establish that an agent's ownership of a libertarian choice is morally significant. It cannot do this, so the objection runs, since a libertarian choice is no different from a chance event, and we do not want to hold individuals morally accountable for actions that happen randomly or by chance. I will refer to this criticism of libertarianism as the Chance Objection, and I will argue in the remainder of this chapter that it is not, in fact, the decisive objection to libertarianism that it initially appears to be.

## When Chance Is Exculpating

The first step that must be taken in evaluating the force of the Chance Objection is that of getting a better handle on the concept of chance as it functions in the argument. Once we have done so, it will then be possible to see whether a libertarian choice is a chance event in precisely that sense of chance that it is antithetical to moral responsibility.

It is, in fact, very difficult to give a precise mathematical or scientific definition of chance. Moreover, the notion of chance that many philosophers, mathematicians, and scientists settle upon calls for a good bit of technical sophistication.[4] This is in contrast to the insight that an event's being a chance event is inconsistent with holding an individual morally responsible. It is an insight that I take to be shared by those who have thought little or not at all about the technical issue of chance. What this suggests is that it is not a technical understanding of chance that is behind our moral intuitions here. Whatever are the salient features of an event viewed as a chance event in this objection, recognition of them may very well not depend on bringing to the discussion a technically refined and philosophically sophisticated grasp of the nature of chance. If one does insist on a fairly technical understanding of chance and randomness, one can handle this objection in fairly short order.[5] To get a handle on what is meant by a chance event as it is taken to apply to libertarian choices, I shall now proceed to isolate those features that make what are loosely called chance events inconsistent with moral responsibility. I start by considering two examples of such chance events.

> A man has been issued a restraining order that requires that he not come within 200 yards of his estranged wife. He purchases box seats at a Toronto Blue Jays baseball game. During the seventh inning stretch, he realizes that his wife is also in attendance and is seated a scant six rows behind him. When she takes him to court for violating the terms of his restraining order, his attorney notes that the man's proximity to his wife at the game was a chance encounter for which he cannot reasonably be held responsible.

> A woman is driving home from the car dealer in her new candy-apple-red convertible when her steering column undergoes a catastrophic malfunction and she veers uncontrollably and crashes into a barbershop. She feels terrible about damaging this poor man's business and offers to pay for damages; however, she rightly does not feel morally responsible because the accident was a freakish or chance occurrence.[6]

Here, then, are two cases in which we would be inclined to characterize an event as a chance event and in which we are consequently inclined to believe that the relevant individual in the two cases is not morally responsible for the respective outcomes. To decide whether libertarian choices are similarly exculpatory chance events, we must decide precisely what it is about the aforementioned scenarios that makes us loathe to assign moral responsibility. Once we have identified the relevant aspects of the situations, we can then decide whether libertarian choices share the same exculpatory features.

There are, it seems to me, two points that are likely to be focused on at the outset. First, it will be said that the aforementioned "chance" outcomes prohibit the assignment of moral responsibility because neither outcome was planned by the individual in question. Second, it will also likely be said that moral responsibility should not be assigned because the outcomes depend upon factors not under the control of the individual in question. Emphasizing the first point, it might be said that the husband did not plan the unfortunate encounter with his wife and that the proud new-car owner did not plan or set out to have her car plow into the barbershop. Emphasizing the second point, it can be said that neither the estranged wife's attendance at the game nor the failure of the steering mechanism was under the control of the individual being exonerated for the outcome. As initially inviting as these approaches may seem, they do not capture with enough specificity what it is about the above scenarios that leads us to identify them as ones in which an individual should not be viewed as morally responsible. Nonetheless, considering precisely why they are not fully adequate will point us to precisely what it is about our two chance events that leads us to exonerate the individuals in question. To see why it is insufficient to say simply that the events were unplanned or dependent upon factors outside of the individual's control, we need only alter the runaway-car scenario by stipulating that the driver was told not to drive the car off the lot that day and was also told the reason that she should not do so; that is, a mechanic had just identified a likely fatal flaw in the vehicle's steering mechanism. In this revised scenario, we do think that it is appropriate to hold the driver morally accountable even though the ensuing accident is still as unplanned as it was in the original. It would still not be true to say that she planned or set out to plow into the barbershop. Likewise, the failure of the steering mechanism is still dependent on factors that are outside of the woman's control. Why the steering column failed when it did had to do in large part with what went on at the manufacturing plant that produced it. So it is that the revised scenario for which we are willing to hold the woman accountable is still one that could be described as unplanned and as dependent on factors outside the woman's control. But now, if we focus on precisely what has changed in the scenario, we will get our clue as to what the crucial feature is that renders the original scenarios ones for which we do not hold the individual in question responsible. What is different about the revised scenario is that the individual now *knows* about the flaw in the steering mechanism and thus is in position to foresee that driving the car away from the lot stands a good chance of resulting in an accident. What this suggests is that the chance event of the careening new car is one for which the individual is not morally culpable because the individual could not have been reasonably expected to foresee the failure of the steering column as a possible outcome of driving the car home. And the same, it seems to me, is true of the restraining order violation. To see this, we can alter the restraining order example by stipulating that the man knows his wife has season tickets to the baseball game and knows where her seats are. Let us also further imagine that the man is offered free tickets to seats that he knows would put him in violation of his restraining order. He really wants to go to the game, but he also wants to respect the terms of the restraining order. After a considerable inner struggle, he decides to go. Now in this case, he did not plan or set out to have an encounter with his wife. What he set out to do was see a thrilling baseball game. Nor is his wife's attendance at the game under his control any more than it was in the preceding example. Nonetheless, we do now feel comfortable saying that the man is morally responsible for violating his restraining order, for we now believe that it was reasonable to expect him to foresee the outcome of his decision to attend. And what this suggests is that the salient feature of the original scenario is that the man did not know where his wife would be sitting or even that she would be attending the game at all. He could not, therefore, have been reasonably expected to foresee that his going to the game would result in his being in such proximity to his wife. It is for this reason that we are unwilling to blame the man for this outcome.

What our analysis of these two cases suggests, then, is that our unwillingness to assign praise or blame for such "chance" events is grounded in the fact that the outcome in such cases is not one that the individual can reasonably have been expected to consider or anticipate in advance. Thus it is that the reasoning behind our intuition that a chance event is one for which an individual should not be held morally responsible would appear to be the following: A chance event is an event that an individual could not reasonably be expected to foresee; it is not appropriate to hold an individual responsible for an event that he or she could not be reasonably expected to foresee; therefore, it is not appropriate to hold an individual morally responsible for a chance event.

Having thus isolated what stands behind the intuition that it is not appropriate to hold an individual morally responsible for chance events, like those described above, we are now in position to ask whether the same exculpatory factors are present in the case of libertarian free choices. We must ask, that is, whether a libertarian free choice is a choice of an action that an individual could not have been reasonably expected to foresee. When we do so ask, it immediately becomes clear that many cases of libertarian free choices do not share the exonerating ignorance present in our examples. In the case of many libertarian free choices, the individual has been deliberating among a set of different possible actions and has wound up selecting one of the possible actions that he contemplated. Thus, unlike the cases of the restraining order and the car crash, a libertarian free choice does not rest on the notion that the choice in question was a possibility that the agent in question could not have reasonably been expected to consider before acting. And even in cases where we imagine the individual to have acted without extensive deliberation in advance, it is still appropriate to say that the individual was aware of the possibility that he would make the choice he did in advance of actually making the choice. The lead time prior to choice and the recognition of it as a possible course of action might be very brief, but if the act is to count as free, it is arguable that it must be one that *(a)* the individual considered before acting and *(b)* the individual had the ability to refrain from performing in the time between conception and execution.

Thus it is that the kind of exculpatory condition at work in our two chance examples is not present in the case of a libertarian choice. Still, this is not yet sufficient as a full reply to the Chance Objection, for the Chance Objector might advance a slightly different case of exculpatory chance that does not allow of the same analysis and which bears a much closer resemblance to a libertarian choice. In the next section I consider such an example.

## Chance and Exculpatory Ignorance

Remember the despicable dad from chapter two, the father who berated his son for being small? He's behaving badly again. This time he's criticizing the little boy's seventeen-year-old brother, who sold the father a losing raffle ticket from a fund-raiser for the high school marching band. "Nice work, Sir Isaac Einstein," the father fumes. "You sold the winning ticket to old Mrs. Gowers across the street. You had the winning ticket. You could have given it to me, but no, you had to include it among the thirty tickets the ol' prune face purchased. As if the Widow Gowers needs a satellite TV system. As if she's gonna even be able to operate the remote control. Here's an idea: Maybe you should try thinking before you act. No, wait: Maybe you should try thinking, period."

Once again we'd be appalled by the man's behavior. And here too, part of what would bother us would be the shallowness of the man's values. But we'd be no less bothered by the fact that he's faulting his son for something that the young man should not be faulted for. The drawing was a random drawing. The fact that the father held a losing ticket was the product, ultimately, of a chance event; therefore, it is not an outcome for which the seventeen-year-old should be held responsible. While this is clearly so, the reason that the randomness of the outcome is an exculpatory fact is not exactly the same as that which was operative in the case of the careening car or the harassing husband. Here, it is not true that the son could not reasonably have been expected to consider the possibility that the ticket he handed his father would turn out to be one of the losing tickets. In this respect, this example of a chance event more closely resembles the case of a libertarian choice than do the previous two examples of chance events. In the case of a libertarian choice, it seems also correct to say that the individual considered various courses of action and yet did not know which course he or she would take prior to actually making a choice. And this parallels the fact that the seventeen-year-old knew that his father's ticket would be either a winner or loser, but did not know which outcome would obtain prior to the spin of the raffle wheel. Since the ignorance is exculpatory in the case of the ill-fated raffle ticket, the ignorance of what libertarian choice one will actually make is also exculpatory. And thus it is that an analysis of an ordinary case of exculpatory chance has revealed that it would not make sense to hold individuals responsible for their libertarian free actions. And this is to say that libertarianism cannot make sense of moral responsibility after all.

## When Ignorance Is Not Exculpating

The Chance Objection to libertarianism has thus evolved into the following: If we do not fault an individual for making the wrong selection in a game of chance, because it would be unreasonable to expect that they know which of a foreseen array of possible outcomes would be the case, then it would be likewise unreasonable to hold an individual responsible for a libertarian choice, for an individual poised before a libertarian choice likewise does not know which choice she will make prior to making it. And this means that libertarianism cannot make sense of moral responsibility and is, therefore, an incoherent account of freedom. This incoherence, moreover, means that the theist cannot avail himself of libertarian freedom in responding to the logical version of the problem of evil. While the story the theist tells in order to respond to the logical version of the problem of evil need not be true or even probably true, the components of the story must at least be coherent. With this, I believe we have arrived at the essence of the insight that is behind what I have called the Chance Objection to libertarianism.

Central to this objection is the notion that the ignorance at work in the raffle example and the libertarian choice are relevantly similar. This, however, is a point at which the objection might be deemed vulnerable, for the libertarian might contend that the ignorance in the two cases differs in important respects. In particular, it might be alleged that the equal probability that each of the raffle wheel's slots is the winning slot is what underpins the ignorance in the case of the raffle example; whereas, ignorance about which choice an individual will make does not presuppose that some choices have no greater probability than others. While this is no doubt true, it is not clear to me that it is of any help to the libertarian. Let us say that there is a 90 percent chance that a recovering alcoholic will fail within the first week. How is this relevant to the freedom of his choosing not to drink should he succeed in doing so? Are we to say that it is somehow less free and less to his credit because the choice made was one that he had less likelihood of making? The libertarian, of course, would want to say no such thing. If anything, the choice not to drink would be more to his credit. Moreover, it seems to me that stressing the *likelihood* of certain actions in responding to this objection is really to concede too much to compatibilism. It is to start to succumb to the notion that accountability makes sense only where we can establish a connection between the action performed and the psychological history of the person who performed it. And this would be to concede that the freedom of a free choice is in direct proportion to the degree to which the free choice is correlated with the person's beliefs, desires, and character traits.

So let us stipulate that the kind of ignorance involved in the two cases is similar in all relevant respects. Before we conclude there-from that libertarian choices involve an element of ignorance that blocks the assignment of moral responsibility, however, there is a further question that must be asked. Having granted that the igno-rance present in the two cases is relevantly the same, we must still ask whether the role that the ignorance plays in the two cases is likewise parallel. To see whether the ignorance functions in the same way in the two cases, it is instructive to ask why the igno-rance in the case of the raffle scenario is exculpating. Once we've asked this question, we are in position to see that it is exculpating because it impedes the individual's ability to produce a specific outcome; that is, selecting the winning slot. That there is no way of knowing which number will be the winner or even likely to be the winner is an ignorance that significantly impedes the agent's ability to pick the winning number. And all this is to say that once the individual was committed to purchasing a ticket, he lacked the knowledge he would have needed to act so as to avoid selecting a losing ticket. Thus it is that there is a sense in which the exculpat-ing nature of chance in the raffle example really reduces to a fail-ure of the action to satisfy the Avoidability Condition. Once again, our despicable dad is chastising a person for something that they could not reasonably have been expected to avoid. Given what it was possible to know, how could the boy have been expected to behave differently so as to avoid the outcome in question?

Now that we have isolated how ignorance functions in the raffle example so as to exculpate the agent, we can now consider whether the ignorance in a libertarian choice functions in the same excul-patory way. We must ask, that is, whether one's ignorance of which choice will be made somehow inhibits one from making a certain choice? The answer to this question, it seems fairly obvious to me, is no. Ignorance concerning which of a possible array of choices one will make does not significantly inhibit one's ability to make any of the possible choices before oneself. Indeed, in the case of a libertarian free choice, the ignorance is a result of the fact that the agent has this special ability to initiate an action. It would, there-fore, hardly make sense to suggest that the ignorance compromises this ability. It is, rather, engendered by the ability. So whereas it is true that the ignorance behind a libertarian choice is similar to that behind the outcome of a game of chance, it is not true that the ignorance in the two cases functions in the same exculpatory way. The reason is that the ignorance inherent in a game of chance does impede one's ability to secure a certain outcome whereas the ignorance preceding a libertarian choice does not impede one's ability to make any of those choices one considers in advance. Indeed, it does not impede one's ability to choose some course of action that only occurred to one in the moment of choice.[7]

## Lingering Libertarian Doubts

There are, then, important differences between chance events and libertarian choices. Specifically, those factors that render chance events ones for which we may not want to hold an individual accountable are not present in libertarian choices. Nonetheless, I know that many readers will be reluctant to grant that libertarian agent causality is a coherent notion. It is a reluctance evident in the sorts of epithets that are routinely applied to libertarian agent causality, epithets such as "bizarre" and "mysterious" and "magical." Indeed, though I here wish to defend the coherence of libertarian agent causality, I too confess to bouts of feeling that there is something fishy about the notion. Some of this lingering suspicion, it seems to me, arises from the following kind of concern. On the libertarian view, prior to performing an action, the person is connected to the array of considered courses of action in the same way; that is, no one of them is he causally determined to perform. And this means that we do not have a complete explanation of why a specific course of action was chosen, for we cannot specify on libertarian assumptions what the crucial factor is that makes one choose the course of action that one does choose. There is, of course, the possibility of explaining why a libertarian choice was made by pointing to a reason for the choice; however, this cannot be counted as a full explanation as to why a particular free choice was made, for there will normally also be reasons against the course of action undertaken. To have such a full explanation, we need more than just a statement of the reason for the choice, for there were any number of reasons at work on the individual prior to his decision. What is needed to complete the explanation is the identification of the decisive factor that led the individual to act on the basis of the reason that informed his choice on this occasion. And it is precisely here, an objector might note, that the explanation remains forever incomplete.

Now it seems to me that the appropriate thing for the libertarian to say at this point is that the much-sought-after decisive factor is nothing other than the person's making a decision. Many, no doubt, will not find this a very satisfying answer, for in some ways it is a repudiation of the question. Where the opponent of libertarianism wants that factor that would explain what brought about a certain choice, the libertarian points simply to the agent's choosing. But is that, after all, such an unsatisfying answer? We have already seen that a libertarian choice is significantly different from those kinds of chance events for which we would not hold an individual responsible. Why do we insist on something more? Having worked through the fact that there is nothing about libertarian choice that is at odds with moral responsibility, I would here suggest that this insistence is misplaced.

Another potential source of unease with the preceding defense of libertarianism might have to do with the manner in which the discussion was conducted. Throughout this chapter I have proceeded as if libertarian choices are made in a controlled and antiseptic laboratory of reasons. The reader may well have envisioned the agent as standing before an array of reasons, coolly evaluating those various reasons, and then making a decision to act upon one of them where the individual's making this decision is not causally influenced by any of the agent's other psychological states—states such as fears, inclinations, desires, and habits. Obviously, such a picture is a distortion. This is not to say that it is a pernicious distortion. Indeed, it has at least two virtues. First, it emphasizes the importance that reasons play in a free choice. Second, it emphasizes the fact that a libertarian choice is not causally determined by any prior factors. It is, thus, an instructive distortion, but it is a distortion nonetheless. What it leaves out of account is the influence that a whole host of psychological states and events do seem to have upon the choices that we make. It is natural to think of desires and emotions, for instance, as exerting a kind of pressure upon us to make certain choices. It is precisely because of such factors that the choices that human beings make are far more predictable than a libertarian account of choice would lead one to expect. Indeed, what the influence of emotions and desires and habits upon our choices and the predictability of these choices suggest is that our choices are causally determined by our psychological makeup, just as the compatibilist had indicated.

While the felt influence of one's psychological makeup on one's choices is strong evidence against what I called the "antiseptic" model of libertarian choice, there are two reasons that I do not think it is strong evidence against libertarian freedom in toto. First, though the influence of such psychological factors as emotions is part of the phenomenology of choice, so is the experience of being able to act in defiance of any and all of the psychological factors that one might identify as influencing one's choice. Thus it is that if we're to trust our experience of what it is like to make a choice, then we should conclude that our libertarian choices are causally influenced but not decisively determined by other psychological factors. The second reason that I don't think this more complicated picture of human choice counts decisively against libertarianism is that it seems to me that this picture of choice is pretty much what one would expect to find in a situation in which choices are made by beings who are both free (in a libertarian sense) and embodied.

## But Are We Free?

I suspect that some will be struck by the fact that virtually all the work done in chapters 2 and 3 has been devoted to showing that libertarianism is a better theory of freedom than is compatibilism, while comparatively little work has been done to defend the contention that human beings are free. Part of the reason for this was dictated by the context in which the discussion of freedom arose. It arose in the course of developing a response to the logical version of the problem of evil. Given that the only requirement on the theist's response is that it be internally coherent, there was no need to prove that human beings were free in a libertarian sense in order to posit this freedom in fashioning a reply to the logical version of the problem of evil. Indeed, there was not even the need to prove that libertarianism is a more plausible account of human freedom than is compatibilism. To the extent that I have succeeded in showing that it is, my defense of libertarianism goes beyond what is strictly required in responding to the logical version of the problem of evil.

There is, however, another reason that I have not offered a detailed argument in defense of believing that human beings are free. The reason is that it seems to me to be the default position in that it has both experience and—what is even more significant—powerful moral intuitions on its side. The experience on its side is that human beings do sometimes feel themselves as having the ability to act in defiance of any set of preceding causes of which they are aware. The moral intuitions it has on its side are the following: (1) it only makes sense to hold human beings responsible for those actions that they perform freely, and (2) it does make sense to hold human beings responsible for some of their actions.

Now having said this, I do not mean to imply that I think it impossible that we are not free. But I do mean to imply that the burden of proof is squarely upon those who would contend that human beings are never free in their actions. And while one might wonder about how strong the appeal to experience is in this case, the weight that most of us are willing to give the aforementioned moral intuitions suggests that any case that one makes for the rejection of freedom must be compelling indeed. Perhaps if science came down on the side of determinism unequivocally, then there might—but even this is far from clear to me—be sufficient grounds for abandoning freedom. But as we noted in the first chapter, science is far from unequivocally embracing a deterministic vision of the universe and human beings.

A theist, then, is quite within her rights to advance libertarian freedom as part of her reply to the logical version of the problem of evil. Moreover, it would be tempting to think that in reaching this point, the theist's work would be done in responding to the charge that theism is logically incoherent. Remarkably, this is not so, for even if the atheist concedes the existence of libertarian freedom, there are still additional questions that she would be well within her rights to want answered before she would finally be forced to admit that the logical version had been solved. What these additional questions are and how the theist might handle them is the subject of the next two chapters.

# Chapter Four

# The Possibility of Moral Perfection

The case that I have been building in response to the logical version of the problem of evil—the free will defense—involves the following two claims: (*a*) moral evil is an ineliminable possible side-effect of God's creation of free beings and (*b*) the world is better by having free beings than it would be if it lacked them. In developing this story against the challenge of the logical version of the problem of evil, the focus thus far has been on showing that the libertarian freedom presupposed by the free will defense is a respectable account of human action. Failing such a defense, the free will defender might be dismissed on the grounds of deploying phantoms in defense of the fantastic. But that much, I believe, we have shown the free will defender not to be guilty of.

There is, however, more work to be done before the logical version of the problem of evil can be set aside. When this logical version was introduced in the first chapter, much was made of the fact that it is the most vulnerable of versions of the problem of evil. All a theist need do to respond to this version of the problem, it was suggested, is sketch a story that is internally consistent and explains how God and any instance of evil might coexist. The theist need not argue that the story is true or even likely to be true. So long as the story is not internally contradictory, the theist will have succeeded in responding to the logical version of the problem of evil. Having noted this vulnerability, however, it was also noted that this vulnerability is partly offset by God's omnipotence, an aspect of God's nature that gives the atheist license to advance any logically possible state of affairs as a route that an omnipotent God could have taken to avoid the production of some instance of evil. The atheist need not argue that the story they tell about how God could have avoided evil is true or even likely to be true. So long as the story is internally consistent, it is an option open to

God. One such option that stands as a serious challenge to the free will defense will be the focus of this chapter.

## Freedom Without Fault

One of the things that libertarian freedom implies is that all occasions on which an individual freely chooses to do evil are occasions on which it would have been possible for the individual to choose to refrain from doing the evil. If this were not a possibility, then the individual's choice would neither be a free choice nor one for which the individual should be held responsible. (Let us not forget, the atheist might say, your defense of the Avoidability Condition in chapter 2.) So libertarian freedom is wedded to the notion that any instance of evil freely done is an instance in which it was possible that the evil not be done. But if it is possible that an individual refrain from doing evil on any occasion in which evil was chosen, then it follows that it is possible that all free agents can refrain from doing evil on all occasions. That this would happen may be very improbable. This need not worry us, however, for the point at issue is not the likelihood that universal forbearance from evil should come to pass. The point is, rather, that such universal forbearance from the performance of evil is a possibility. So it is, the atheist may argue, that the existence of a realm of free beings who choose unfailingly to refrain from evil is a possibility. And thus it is that even the free will defense does not excuse God for the moral evil in the universe, for it must be conceded that a universe of free beings who never do evil is a logical possibility.[1] And this means that we've described a possible world that would have been better than the actual world that God did create. And this means that either God does not have the power to bring it about (in which case the theist must back off of God's omnipotence) or God did not know how to bring it about (in which case the theist must back off of God's omniscience) or God did not want to bring it about (in which case the theist must back off of God's omnibenevolence). Whichever way the theist goes, the theist will have to reject one of the traditional attributes of God;

and this means that even moral evil cannot be reconciled with God's existence. So the contradiction between God and evil does not disappear even if we buy the defense of libertarian freedom sketched in the preceding chapters.

Thus it is, the atheist might say, that two can play the game of sketching stories that are logically consistent. Before the theist can declare the free will defense a success, he must explain why God did not bring about the logical possibility just described. Why didn't God create that possible world in which all free creatures just happen to always choose not to do evil? It is a challenge of daunting simplicity, made all the more formidable because it turns upon a crucial ingredient in the free will defense: the contention that freedom entails the ability to do otherwise. In the next section, however, I will argue that it is a challenge that depends upon a kind of trick. The trick is that the consistency of the atheist's story is only apparent, an apparent consistency born of the fact that the atheist's story is incomplete.

## Impossible Possibilities

That all free beings always freely refrain from evil is logically possible; however, it does not follow that it is logically consistent to suppose that God could cause this to be the case. To see that this is so, it is important to note that "having been created by God" is an important fact about any **state of affairs** that God does create. This is what the objection leaves out of account and by doing so creates the illusion of logical possibility. Thus it is that it might be possible for there to be a state of affairs that is internally consistent, and yet it is not consistent to suppose that it is created by God, for the addition of the fact that the state of affairs is created by God may be inconsistent with some fact about the state of affairs. For example, it is logically possible that there be something that is in no way dependent upon anything else. (For many theists, in fact, God is such a being.) Nonetheless, it is logically impossible that God create something that is independent of all other things, for the fact of its being created entails that it is dependent upon the creator for its existence. So while it is not contradictory to suppose that there be such a radically independent thing, it is contradictory to suppose that such a radically independent thing be created. And thus it is that there can be some state of affairs that is internally consistent and yet impossible to create. But if it is contradictory to suppose that such a thing be created, then God's inability to create the thing is no limit on God's omnipotence, for God's omnipotence extends only as far as the logically possible.

A slightly different—and perhaps more accurate—way to put this point is to note that when one is contemplating whether a state of affairs can possibly be brought about, it is not enough to simply look at the state of affairs without reference to the fact of its being done. This is because the fact of its being done is a fact about the state of affairs. Thus whenever we ask whether God can create some state of affairs, we must recognize that God's creation of the state of affairs is one of the facts that must be considered in deciding whether the proposed state of affairs is logically contradictory.

Here's an imperfect though, I hope, illuminating analogy. It is possible that I could be carried away by others; however, it is not possible that I would be the one who does the carrying. This is not for want of strength, for we may suppose that I am capable of carrying a person twice my size. Nor is it because one cannot carry oneself, for I'm sure that clever analytic philosophers raised on a steady diet of thought experiments could devise some scenario in which we would be inclined to say that one carried oneself. It is simply because the act in question, being carried away by others, though consistent in itself, cannot consistently be supposed to have been done only by me. The fact of my doing the carrying would contradict the component of the act that specifies that others do the carrying. Notice also that we would balk at the suggestion that my inability to perform the act of my being carried away by others is an inability that reflects on a lack of power, for the action to be performed—though consistent in itself—is not one that can be consistently done by me.

Now if we return to the possible world in which all free agents always refrain from doing evil, we must note that God's creating this world is one of the facts that must be reconciled with all the others. But it is clear that for God to cause such a world to come into being would require that God do something more than create free creatures and then hope that everything turns out well. For God's doing this is consistent with the world turning out as it actually did turn out; namely, a realm in which free beings routinely use their freedom to do evil. No, for God to create a world in which it was guaranteed that free beings would never use their freedom to do evil, God would have to ensure that those beings never use their freedom to do evil. But given that God's will cannot be resisted—this is part of God's omnipotence—it follows that God's ensuring that human beings never freely choose evil entails that those human beings could not freely choose evil. And this, of course, is the point at which the incoherence of the atheist's challenge is revealed; for it involves the demand that God create beings who are free in a libertarian sense and yet are unable to do evil. But it is part of the libertarian conception of freedom that a human being be able to choose evil as well as good. Therefore, it is logically contradictory to suppose that God could have created free beings who inevitably did only good and never evil. So while a world in which all free beings always refrain from evil is internally possible, it is not possible for such a world to be created, for its being made would contradict the libertarian freedom that is part of the description of the world. This is the crucial detail that the atheist left out and thereby created the illusion that it would be logically consistent to suppose that God create a world of free creatures who are morally perfect.[2]

Still, the atheist might not be ready to relent. What you say is true enough, the atheist's complaint might begin, it would be contradictory for God to directly create a world in which all the free beings are caused by Him to always refrain from doing evil. But now who is guilty of telling an incomplete story? Surely as supreme a being as God would have options other than direct force to achieve his aims. Surely a being of infinite wisdom could figure out a way to finesse the situation, to cajole and prod his free beings in just those ways that only He knows will result in their freely choosing not to do evil.

## Finessing Human Freedom

The task of planning a family reunion has fallen to you. This requires that you find some way of preventing Uncle Billy from
wreaking his usual havoc at such events. Uncle Billy, you see,
doles out insults for sport. Not good-natured barbs, mind you, but
nasty insults that cut to the core of another's vulnerability and
tend to start fights. You've noticed, however, that if Uncle Billy
brings his banjo, he's a different man, a man so consumed with
entertaining that starting fights is the furthest thing from his mind.
Thus it is that you write a special note on Billy's invitation: "Please
bring your banjo." But Billy is forgetful, so you borrow a banjo
from a friend just to make sure that come party time Uncle Billy
will be pickin' and grinnin' instead of grousin' and sinnin.'

What's noteworthy about your plan is that you have prevented
Uncle Billy from doing evil without compromising his freedom.
You did not coerce or directly cause him to refrain from his mis-
chief (as was done at your wedding reception when Billy was
locked in the tool shed at the start of the festivities); nonetheless,
you took appropriate steps to see to it that Billy would be in an
environment in which he would freely choose to refrain from evil.
And this, your ability to take noncoercive measures to guide human beings away from evil, is the source of a challenge for the
theist. It may well be wondered whether the free will defense can
really exonerate God for the moral evil in the universe when God
might have done precisely what you did in the case of Uncle Billy.
Why couldn't an omniscient God have known what use free creatures would make of their freedom in various circumstances and
then used this knowledge to select that world in which circumstances were tailored so as to ensure that all free creatures would
consistently but freely refrain from doing evil? Thus it is that the
free will defense, even where freedom is construed in libertarian
terms, does not excuse God for creating a world that allows for the
possibility of moral evil. And just as you've arranged for circumstances in which Billy will freely refrain from evil, why couldn't God—
who is both much wiser and more powerful than you—arrange

circumstances in which all free beings would always freely refrain from doing evil without it being the case that God directly
causes the free beings to refrain from performing evil deeds. Surely
God knows the tendencies of free beings much better than you;
therefore, it should be no great challenge to God to create circumstances in which those free beings don't perform evil deeds. And
this is relevant to the charge of incoherence that was leveled against
the suggestion that God bring about that possible world in which
all free beings consistently and freely refrain from doing evil. That
charge of incoherence, the atheist might now object, rested on the
assumption that God could only ensure that humans would refrain
from evil by directly causing them to do so, a direct causing that
would compromise the libertarian freedom they are alleged to have.
But now we see that God could have ensured that human beings
would never go wrong without directly causing them to do anything and without thereby compromising their freedom to do evil.
God puts human beings in situations in which they could do evil
and does not prevent their doing it, but knows the human beings in
question so well that the circumstances in which he places them
are ones in which they are simply not going to choose to do evil. If
you can pull this off with your Uncle Billy, then surely God can do
it with the rest of us.[3]

But there are two things to note about the Uncle Billy scenario.
The first is that it ascribes a much higher predictability to free
human behavior than seems to me to be the case. This is not to say
that human beings do not display marked tendencies to behave in
certain ways. It is to say, however, that it is unrealistic to have
anything other than a modest confidence in our ability to predict
what others and even what we ourselves will do on a given occasion. My own experience is that people often react in ways other
than I anticipate. There have been times when I dreaded having to
pass criticism on to an individual of an extremely volatile tem-
perament, only to have the individual take the criticism with ad-
mirable restraint and grace. On other occasions, I have been
shocked by the reaction of a generally sweet-tempered individual
to news that I thought rather trivial. The second thing it is worth

noting about the Uncle Billy scenario is that to the extent that we justifiably have confidence in our predictions about free human behavior, this is normally because we are dealing with individuals who have a fairly long history of free decisions that we can consult, a history of decisions that has led to the individual's development of certain tendencies or character traits. This, of course, is the very old story of virtues and vices as habits, habits that are produced—in large part—by the individual's past behavior. As was mentioned near the end of chapter 3, there is no inconsistency in holding both of the following: Some human actions are free in a libertarian sense, and repeated free actions can form habits where these habits make it difficult to act otherwise. Indeed, there is even nothing inconsistent between ascribing libertarian freedom to an individual and maintaining that an individual may eventually forfeit that freedom because of the history of her or his free decisions. Whether this actually happens, I am in no position to say; however, it does not seem at all inconsistent with a libertarian account of freedom to suppose that it is something that one might lose. Now, if this is the model of libertarian freedom that we are working with—and it would fly in the face of common sense to dismiss the doctrine of character formation—then what needs to be noted is that God's position in creating a certain world is actually very different from the position you would be operating from when you make sure that you have a banjo at the reunion. Unlike you, God does not have a history of the free decisions that a human being will make. And if the doctrine of character formation just sketched makes sense, then it follows that even God does not know independently of an individual's actual decisions what the individual's character will be. This character itself is largely a product of the free choices that an individual makes. Therefore, in contemplating what kind of world to produce, God does not have access to precisely that information that would be needed to produce a world in which all human beings refrain from ever doing evil.

But the atheist may concede that the Uncle Billy scenario is an imperfect analogy for the kind of thing she is demanding of God. Indeed, she is likely to identify yet another disanalogy, for there is an important difference between the two cases that only serves to deepen the theist's predicament.

## What Does Omniscience Know?

God is not simply more knowledgeable than we are; God is alleged to be perfectly knowing or all-knowing. Perhaps the uncertainty in our own projections of what a person will freely do are a result of the fact that we are far from omniscient. And perhaps we also need not be concerned about our reliance upon an individual's developed character when we make predictions about his or her behavior. Perhaps our need to do so is again simply a reflection of the extreme finitude of our intellects. Given that God is operating under no such constraints, it might be the case that God has no need to appeal to an individual's developed character in order to know what that individual will freely do under certain circumstances, and this means that God would know the first free choices of a being that has, as yet, no character forged on a history of choices. If God can know such matters, then it seems that the theist still has some explaining to do before the logical version of the problem of evil can be set aside. If God can know such matters, it would have amounted to gross negligence for God not to have relied upon this knowledge in creating the world.

The suggestion developed at the end of the preceding section is that an all-knowing God can know what a free being would do under any set of hypothetical circumstances. This knowledge, if there is such, includes at least two distinct kinds of cases. One of these would be God's ability to know what a person would have done under circumstances that did not obtain. Here, the question is whether God knows propositions of the following form: If person X had been placed in circumstances Y, then X would have freely done Z. Such statements are sometimes called **counterfactuals of freedom**. They are counterfactuals because they speculate about what would have happened had the facts been other than they were. They speculate, that is, about matters that are counter to the facts. They are said to be counterfactuals of freedom, because the speculation in this case is about what an individual would have freely done under circumstances other than those that did obtain. The other kind of knowledge God might be thought to have about the behavior of free beings under hypothetical circumstances would be God's knowing what a person will freely do in certain circumstances when it is not yet determined whether the person will be in those circumstances. In the latter case, the question is whether God can know the truth of propositions of the form: If person X is placed in circumstances Y, then X will freely do Z. Statements of this form are often called **deliberative conditionals**. They are conditionals because they assert that one state of affairs is a sufficient condition for a second. They are deliberative in that one might consult such conditionals in deliberating about whether or not to undertake a certain course of action.

God's knowing whether propositions such as these are true or false is sometimes called **middle knowledge** (*scientia media*). This term—which seems to have been coined by sixteenth-century philosopher and theologian Luis de Molina—reflects the notion that such knowledge is intermediate between God's knowledge of actual events and God's knowledge of a range of mere possibilities.[4] Insofar as counterfactuals deal with what might have been and deliberative conditionals with what is not yet, they are short of God's knowledge of actual events or actual states of affairs. God's knowing such propositions, on the other hand, would be fuller knowledge than that involved in knowing the full range of possibilities that a free creature might choose in a certain set of circumstances. God certainly does have knowledge of all the possibilities open to a free creature under given circumstances, but if God has middle knowledge, then God has something more than this. If God has middle knowledge, God knows precisely which of the range of possibilities a free creature will in fact choose. A chess master who knew all the legal moves her opponent could make under any given configuration of pieces would certainly know the full range of possibilities that could unfold in a game. But the chess master would have something more if she also knew precisely which of those legal moves her opponent would freely make under each of the game's possible conditions. Such a chess master would have middle knowledge.

As is often the case in philosophical discussions, the flow of the argument has dictated the content of the discussion and has pushed the discussion onto terrain quite different from that on which it started. In the present chapter, we began with a challenge to the free will defense that had God's omnipotence as its centerpiece. In the course of developing a response to that challenge, the free will defender suddenly finds himself faced with another challenge, a challenge in which God's omniscience has taken center stage. Given that God's omniscience would include all middle knowledge, the atheist will want to know why God didn't draw upon this middle knowledge to noncoercively create a universe of free creatures who never use their freedom to do evil. Why didn't God use his knowledge to finesse the problem of moral evil? In the next chapter we will consider two possible answers that the free will defender might give to this question.

*Chapter Five*

# The Matter of Middle Knowledge

As was noted in the last chapter, middle knowledge refers to two different kinds of conditional propositions. The first of these, what are sometimes called counterfactuals of freedom, are statements about what a free being would have done had conditions been other than they were. Though the terminology may sound a bit alien, we assert counterfactuals of freedom all the time. It is accepted political wisdom these days that if President Clinton had admitted his affair with Monica Lewinsky from the beginning, then the House of Representatives would never have voted to impeach him. This is a counterfactual of freedom in that it makes a claim about what free beings—the members of the House of Representatives in this case—would have chosen to do had the facts been other than (counter to) what they actually were.

The second kind of conditional propositions mentioned in the last chapter are deliberative conditionals. These conditionals are statements about what a free being will do in circumstances that are not presently actual but may be actual at some later point. They differ from counterfactuals of freedom in that their speculation is not counter to the facts. Though not currently actual, the condition about which they speculate may well come to pass. Indeed, this is why such conditionals can play an important role in deciding what to do. "If we invite Janet's ex-husband to the party, then she will flirt with him to make her current husband jealous." This is a deliberative conditional that one might rely on in deciding not to invite Janet's ex-husband to the party. And that is the reason they are sometimes called "deliberative" conditionals; they can play an important role in deliberating about what to do.

Though both counterfactuals of freedom and deliberative conditionals would count as middle knowledge, it is really the latter that are directly relevant to our discussion of the logical version of the problem of evil. What we are interested in knowing is whether God could have known with certainty in advance of creating the universe how specific free creatures would behave under any given set of circumstances. If God does have such middle knowledge of deliberative conditionals, then it is perfectly legitimate to wonder why God didn't use this knowledge to create a world in which the free beings He created would always freely refrain from doing evil.

One way of attacking this problem, and the way that I favor, is to approach it head on; that is, deny that there is such a thing as middle knowledge. If God does not know with certainty what course of action a given free creature will take under conditions not yet actual, then even God is not in position to arrange circumstances so as to guarantee that free creatures will always freely refrain from doing evil. If there is no middle knowledge, it would seem that even divinely laid plans may go the way of those laid by mice and men. The trick to this theistic defense, of course, is to find a way to reject middle knowledge without compromising God's omniscience. This, in turn, means arguing that the relevant deliberative conditionals lack a truth value. This is demanded by the nature of omniscience, for omniscience requires—at a minimum—that God know the truth value of every proposition that has a truth value. Thus it is that the only way to legitimately deny that God has middle knowledge is to deny that the relevant conditionals have a truth value, for if deliberative conditionals and counterfactuals of freedom do lack truth value, it is no more a limitation on God's knowledge that he not know their truth values than it would be a limitation on God's knowledge not to know the name of the planet between Earth and Mars. Fortunately for this approach, there is good reason to doubt that deliberative conditionals and counterfactuals of freedom could have a truth value.

## Conditionals Without Truth

The first thing that must be noted to see why it is reasonable to have doubts about middle knowledge is the following: Delibera-

tive conditionals cannot be true or false in virtue of their agree-
ment or disagreement with actual events. They cannot be so for
the simple reason that they do not describe events that are as yet
actual. If a deliberative conditional is true or false, it must be in
virtue of the connection between the state of affairs expressed in
the antecedent and the state of affairs expressed in the consequent.
In fact, the truth or falsity of many conditional statements is
grounded in precisely this way, for such conditionals would be
taken as true or false depending upon the presence or absence of
the logical or causal connection between the antecedent and the
consequent. And if deliberative conditionals are to have a truth
value, it is plausible to suppose that this truth value must be
grounded in some sort of logical or causal connection between the
antecedent and the consequent.

That deliberative conditionals would have their truth values—
if any they have—in a connection between the antecedent and
consequent is further emphasized when we consider how such
conditionals could be of use to God. If deliberative conditionals
are to be of any use to God, they must be asserting that there is
some connection between the antecedent and the consequent such
that the truth of the antecedent *guarantees* that the consequent
also be true. Only thus would God have a reason to actualize the
antecedent in order to indirectly bring about the truth of the consequent. Given that there must be some connection between the antecedent and consequent, however, it is incumbent upon the
advocates of middle knowledge to indicate the nature of this connection. Right away it should be clear that it can neither be a logical nor a causal connection, for either of these would compromise
the freedom of the act specified by the consequent of the
counterfactual.[1] It will not, on the other hand, sufficiently ground
middle knowledge if it is supposed that the connection between
the antecedent and the consequent is merely a probable connection, for this would be consistent with God's plans—at least those
that rest on such counterfactuals—going astray.

Now it might be thought a weakness of the foregoing argument
that it focuses only on logical and causal connections as possible

bases on which to ground the truth value of deliberative conditionals. There are, the objector might note, other possible relations between the antecedent and consequent of a conditional that can ground the truth value of the conditional. Some conditionals, for instance, are grounded in a semantic connection between the antecedent and consequent. "If James is married, then James is not a bachelor" might be counted among such conditionals. This is an example of a true conditional where the truth of the conditional is grounded in the fact that the term "bachelor" includes the characteristic of being unmarried as part of its meaning. Given that there are thus other possible connections between the antecedent and the consequent that might ground its truth value, one must concede that one of these other possible bases might ground the truth value of a deliberative conditional without compromising the freedom that a deliberative conditional includes as part of its consequent.

That this possibility was left open by the argument given above is certainly true; however, there is good reason to be very doubtful that any other possible connection could be up to the task of establishing a truth value for a deliberative conditional without compromising the freedom presupposed by the consequent. Whatever connection between the antecedent and consequent one uses to ground the truth value of a deliberative conditional, it must fall into one of the two following general categories: *(a)* the connection between the antecedent and the consequent is such that the consequent follows from the antecedent with probability but not certainty or *(b)* the connection between the antecedent and consequent is such that the consequent follows upon the antecedent with certainty. Now if the former is the case concerning deliberative conditionals, then it is possible that God could rely on such conditionals in creating the world and yet still have His hopes and plans thwarted. But if the latter is the case, then the problem becomes that of salvaging the freedom presupposed by the consequent. What, that is to say, possible story could one tell in which the consequent follows of necessity from the antecedent and yet in which it was true to say that the action performed in the consequent was such that it might not have been done even given the antecedent? Though I have no general argument to show that there could be no such account, I am highly dubious that one is in the offing. Barring any such story, therefore, we are in our rights to conclude that there is no connection between the antecedent and the consequent that would ground the truth value of a deliberative conditional.

Finally, it might be suggested that the truth of a counterfactual of freedom is simply a fact of the matter that just happens to be true. That X would freely perform Y in circumstances Z is simply something that would happen under those circumstances; however, this being so is not grounded in any independent connection between the state of affairs expressed in the antecedent and that expressed in the consequent. There is no asking why it would happen on this account, it just would; that's just the fact of the matter.

Now this, it seems to me, is the most promising line to take in making sense of the truth value of a deliberative conditional, for it looks initially as though it might allow one to attempt to sidestep the dilemma that was at the center of the argument against middle knowledge developed in the preceding section. As no independent connection has been asserted between the antecedent and consequent, there is no danger of the connection being either *(a)* only probably true and thus unreliable or *(b)* necessarily true and thus at odds with the libertarian freedom presupposed by the consequent. Despite its initial appeal, however, this account also runs into trouble. It has us committed to what turns out to be a very peculiar kind of fact.

What we have on the presently suggested way of salvaging middle knowledge is, in effect, two rival possible worlds before God. In one of those worlds (W) X does Y in Z, and in the other (W*) X does not do Y in Z. These worlds are otherwise similar, at least up until the point at which X finds himself in circumstances Z. And this means that the counterfactual "if God places X in Z, then X will do Y" (henceforth DB) is true in W but not in W*. Now God does not—under pain of contradiction—have the power to directly cause W instead of W* to come about, for such direct causation would compromise the stipulated freedom of X's doing Y.

Nor does God have the power to directly cause W* instead of W to come about, and this for the same reason; namely, God's doing so would compromise the stipulated freedom of X's refraining from Y. But if we suppose that God has middle knowledge, then we must suppose that God simply knows what X will do under circumstances Z. Thus it is that God can use middle knowledge to bring it about that W will occur by willing all those states of affairs in which W and W* overlap. Since circumstances Z are present in both W and W*, God need only create all those states of affairs shared by W and W* and X will take care of the rest, choosing to Y under circumstances Z. Thus it is, according to Alvin Plantinga, that God could indirectly actualize W.

But before we accept this story as coherent, we must ask precisely what is the deliberative conditional that would enable God to know that his actualization of those states of affairs shared by W and W* will lead to the actualization of W and not W*. It would, of course, have to be none other than DB. But it can't be the DB that is true in W, for then God's deciding between W and W* would simply be his directly selecting for W's actuality, and this would contravene the freedom of the act specified by the consequent. It was, we must remember, stipulated that God is not directly responsible for W's coming about instead of W*; however, if the truth of DB is dependent upon God's deciding for it to be true, then God is really the source of the connection between the antecedent and the consequent. Thus it must be that DB is somehow true independently of any possible worlds in which it is true; however, if that is the case then it seems that there is a constraint independent of W and W* concerning which of the worlds can be actualized. But if there is such a constraint, then it would seem that W* is really not a possible world after all. Of course, we might try to respond to this problem by saying that the counterfactuals of freedom are true without being true in any possible world. But as soon as we had said this, I hope we would take it as a hint that we were not on the right track.

In the end, then, I am unable to see what it is that God would know in knowing a counterfactual of freedom. And this is because it seems that the only thing that can settle the truth value of statements about specific free choices on a libertarian account of freedom would be the actual free choices that the person makes. And if this is the only thing that can fix the truth value of propositions about specific free choices, then it follows by definition that the truth of the antecedent of a counterfactual of freedom cannot guarantee the truth of the consequent where the consequent describes a free act; and this means that a counterfactual of freedom cannot be true, as a matter of definition. And if the truth value of a counterfactual of freedom is indeterminate, then it is surely not possible for God to have determinate knowledge of what its truth value is. Indeed, to insist that God knows it determinately when it does not have a determinate truth value would be to render God imperfect, for it would have God believing something that isn't so.[2]

Now there may well be theists who simply do not see the difficulties that I have alleged to befall middle knowledge. Such theists can take comfort from the fact that rejecting middle knowledge is not the only way to respond to the objection it enables the antitheist to pose against the free will defense. There is another way that has been developed by one of the staunchest contemporary defenders of middle knowledge. It is the way of Alvin Plantinga's doctrine of transworld depravity.

## Alvin Plantinga and Transworld Depravity

Imagine that you are responsible for writing the first two-thirds of a novel, with the remaining third being left to someone else, a someone who has the freedom to finish the novel as he sees fit. There are, of course, some constraints upon what he may do in bringing the work to a close. For instance, he cannot suddenly and without explanation shift the setting from Gods Lake, in Manitoba, to a lush purple planet on the outskirts of the Andromeda constellation. Or again, he cannot alter the laws of nature that you have assumed to be operative throughout. But other than these rather general constraints, your coauthor has significant creative liberty. He can kill off whom he chooses, write the moral corruption or

redemption of whomever he chooses, or fashion a romance between (or among if he really wants to boost sales) whomever he
chooses. Now let us further stretch our story by imagining that
even though you cannot directly control how your coauthor will
finish the story, you do know that he will write certain endings if
you provide him with a certain story line. It's not that he's compelled to do so, it's just that you know what he's going to write.
Now let us assume that you write the first two-thirds as a mis-
matched buddy novel in which a cynical and world-weary physi-
cian finds new meaning in life by going hunting in Gods Lake
Manitoba with a fellow doc whom he detests. Your coauthor can
end the novel either happily or tragically. In fact, you hope that he
will end it happily, but it is possible that if you write the story line you
have in mind, your coauthor will have the buddies turn their high-
powered rifles on one another, the book ending with a chillingly detailed description of their frozen corpses being covered by the
winter's first snowfall. You know you dare not begin a novel in
which a woman is married to a good but boring man and then is
liberated and taken on a journey of self-discovery by a mysterious
stranger who blows into town. Why, you know that even using the
term "self-discovery" in a positive way will surely prompt your
coauthor to write an ending of gut-wrenching debauchery, despair,
and betrayal. But now let us be clear about one thing, there is
something that your coauthor will do. He will either end the book
happily or tragically. And this means that whatever he decides to
do was the only novel that you could have participated in bringing
about by starting the novel as you did. If we imagine that you
know how your coauthor will end all the various novels you might
begin and that you can take this knowledge into account in deciding how to begin the novel, then you are roughly in the position
that God would be in if He had middle knowledge and could use
this knowledge in deciding which universe of free beings to create. God's act of creation would start the story of the universe, and
the free decisions of the universe's free creatures would finish the
story; however, God would know in advance how they would use
their freedom in finishing it.

Let us add a further wrinkle to the coauthor scenario. Let us suppose that no matter what story line you begin with, your coauthor is going to find a way to pervert it, at least in part. You set the stage with clowns, balloons, and cotton candy, and your coauthor constructs a second half in which the clowns use the balloons and cotton candy to distribute crack cocaine to schoolchildren. You begin with a tender tale of dew-kissed roses born of the delicate touch of a grandmother's wrinkled hands, and he ends it by having her grandson clip those same roses to be left as calling cards on the victims he murders. No matter how you begin it, your coauthor will introduce some measure of darkness. Under this supposition, it would be true that the only novels you might coauthor would be ones that will contain at least a certain amount of evil. Thus, even though it is strictly speaking possible that a novel of unblemished goodness be written; you have no way of seeing to it that such a novel be written. There is nothing logically or even physically impossible about your coauthor completing the novel benignly. Still, the fact of the matter is that there is no way you can bring about any of those novels. Such is the price of allowing the outcome of your creative enterprise to be partly at the mercy of the free decisions of another.

Plantinga's strategy for exonerating God from the existence of moral evil even under the supposition of middle knowledge is, roughly, to suggest that it is logically possible that in deciding which world of free beings to create, God may be in roughly the same position as you in deciding which book to begin when you know that your coauthor will end it badly. God can choose to create a certain kind of world with a certain natural order and populated with certain free beings, but then God leaves it largely up to those free beings how the moral history of that world will be written. Just as it was supposed to be the case that no matter what kind of novel you began, your coauthor would write an ending filled with at least some unhappiness, so it may be that no matter what kind of world God created directly, at least some of the free beings that populated the world would introduce moral evil into the world's history. The free beings of all possible worlds may suffer, that is, from what Plantinga calls transworld depravity. That is to say, it may be the case that no matter which world and which free beings God decided to create directly, it would always happen that those free beings would in fact behave badly—at least sometimes—in the actual world that God produced.[3]

## Expanding the Logical Version of the Problem of Evil

Either way one goes on the issue of middle knowledge, the use of the free will defense to respond to the abstract logical version of the problem of evil stands. Still, even if the free will defense is sound as a response to the abstract logical version of the problem of evil, it can hardly be taken to constitute a complete response to the challenge that evil poses to theism. While the free will defense may be up to the task of showing that belief in God is consistent with the existence of at least some moral evil, it does not—at least as stated thus far—do anything to show that belief in God's existence can be squared with the natural evil that plagues our world. For that matter, it does not even show that belief in God's existence can be squared with the extravagant amount of moral evil in the world or the horrific nature of some of the things that human beings freely and all too gleefully do to one another. It is one thing to grant that God's existence is consistent with at least some of the moral evil in the universe, but it is an entirely different matter to show that God's existence is consistent with the full domain of moral evil or with any natural evil whatsoever. And once the opponent of theism gets more specific about the quantity and quality of evil in the universe, he is then ready to resurrect the logical version of the problem of evil by contending not that God's existence is inconsistent with any evil whatsoever, but only that God's existence is inconsistent with certain specific kinds and quantities of evil that are part of our world. By simply being more precise about the evil that poses a problem for theism, the advocate of the logical version of the problem of evil has given the theist an additional set of challenges.

Fortunately for the theist, this revised version of the logical problem of evil can be dealt with in fairly short order. As far as the quantity of moral evil goes, one might employ either of two different strategies, depending on whether one believes that God has middle knowledge. For those who reject middle knowledge, it is open to say that the world's containing as much moral evil as it does was an inevitable risk of God's creating a world with a significant number of free beings. For those who buy into middle knowledge, it is open to say that perhaps all those realizable possible worlds that have less moral evil than this world would be worlds that also have significantly less moral good, a trade-off that would render those worlds morally inferior to our world. And as far as the horrific nature of some moral evil is concerned, one might argue that risking such atrocious deeds is the inevitable price of creating free creatures who have the good of substantial—and not merely token—freedom. Any steps that God might have taken to guarantee that no atrocities ever take place might well be steps that would also demand concessions on the significance of human freedom that would denude the world of much of its most cherished goods.

Handling the full gamut of instances of moral evil is thus a simple matter of amplifying the strategies introduced to handle the abstract logical problem of evil. But showing that natural evil is consistent with belief in God's existence is a bit trickier for the simple reason that the existence of natural evils is not—at least on the surface—an inevitable risk involved in the creation of free human beings. Though one might argue that at least some cases of natural evil might be occasions for even greater goods that otherwise would not be—here one might think of acts of self-sacrifice, charity, and compassion undertaken in times of natural disasters—some cases of natural evil stubbornly resist this suggestion. After all, there are undoubtedly far more cases of animal suffering that we are completely unaware of than those that we encounter. I imagine that an average day in a hectare of Amazonian rain forest, hidden from human eyes, contains a grim helping of painful struggles that do not end well for at least one of the creatures involved. There are, for that matter, likely far more cases of animal suffering that occurred before there were any human beings than there are cases of animal sufferings of which we are directly aware. Even Diplodocus had dire days.

But while it may be hard to understand how anywhere near the full range of natural evils could be incorporated into a free will defense that features the freedom of human beings, there is no reason that we need confine ourselves to the belief that human beings are the only free beings created by God. Many religions profess the existence of free spirits, the most common varieties of which are angels and demons. And when we recognize the possibility that there are demons, there would seem to be no definitive reason not to further concede that such malevolent spirits might delight in wreaking havoc on the natural order in such a way that significant suffering is inflicted upon the earth's sentient inhabitants. On this line of thought, the concept of natural evil might be something of a misnomer, for diseases and natural disasters would actually be the vicious deeds of corrupt spirits and thus would be the morally significant consequences of free beings.[4]

But if this line of defense is a touch too occult for your tastes— though it is hard to see how this would disqualify a defense when the only grounds for disqualifying the defense are logical incoherence—there are other avenues open to the apologist that do not depend upon conceding the existence of angels and demons. For those cases of suffering that the natural order inflicts on sentient beings that are not moral agents, it is worth noting that we cannot be absolutely certain that such beings actually do suffer. What we know of infants and lower animals is that they wail and yelp and engage in countless other recognizable signs of suffering, but this does not give us conclusive grounds for believing that such beings actually experience suffering. That such beings do not suffer is not a possibility that we give any weight in our dealings with them. To do so would be to neglect all the evidence we have that such sufferings really do take place. To do so would be to dampen what are clearly desirable humanitarian impulses and sentiments. But the fact remains that there would seem to be nothing barring an omnipotent being from bringing it about that these animals do not really experience the suffering that their behavior otherwise suggests. Actors routinely portray sufferings that they suffer not. Surely an omnipotent being would find it but a small feat to bring it about that the sufferings of all submoral sentient beings, though full of sound and fury, really signify nothing; nothing internal that is. And as for the sufferings inflicted by nature on moral agents, it may well be the case that all such sufferings are at least occasions for moral and spiritual growth. Whether the free beings in question seize upon these opportunities is another matter, but we certainly cannot complain that God has taken all necessary measures to allow His free creatures to succeed in those two most important of arenas, the moral and spiritual.

At this point I imagine a chorus of readers will cry out, "Enough! Though such defenses are logically consistent with theism and the facts about evil, they are so improbable as to defy rational consent." To which the reply is "perhaps they are wildly improbable, but that is beside the point." That a defense is wildly improbable does not disqualify its ability to address a version of the logical problem of evil. Disqualification of a defense to the logical problem of evil would have to take the form of showing that the defense either *(a)* is internally contradictory or *(b)* contradicts some other proposition that is necessarily true. As far as I can see, there is no good reason to suspect that any of the defenses discussed thus far fail to pass either of these tests.

But this victory for theism is both hollow and short-lived. It is hollow because it is a victory largely born of the fact that the logical problem of evil sets itself an almost impossibly high standard of success. It is short-lived because the resurrection of the problem of evil requires only that advocates of the problem soften their inordinately high standards for success. Instead of striving to show that theism and evil are logically contradictory, they need only express the thrust of the problem as that of showing that the evils of our world render it unreasonable to believe in God, where unreasonability of a belief is taken to mean that it is more likely to be false than true. And to see that this gives the advocate of the problem significantly more room to move, it is important to note that the realm of the reasonable is much more extensive than the realm of the logically contradictory. That Elvis is still alive, that I was a victim of an alien abduction not witnessed by others and of which I have no recollection, and that I have fairly dealt myself twenty consecutive royal flushes are all logically possible states of affairs. They are also states of affairs that it would be unreasonable to believe are the case. The mere fact that it cannot be shown that theism and evil are logically inconsistent does not spare theism from the charge that it is on a par with the aforementioned improbable states of affairs. And to show the unreasonableness of theism, it is not necessary to show that evil renders it as implausible as fairly dealing oneself twenty consecutive royal flushes. Indeed, for evil to render theism unreasonable, it need only show that theism is less likely than it is likely.

In the past twenty years or so, such a recasting of the ambitions of the problem of evil is precisely what has taken place.[5] Advocates of the problem of evil have largely abandoned the attempt to show that evil renders theism logically incoherent and have turned their attention to showing that evil renders belief in God's existence more likely to be false than true. And thus it is that a complete response to the problem of evil cannot be content with merely showing that theism and evil are logically consistent. It must address the charge that theism can be upheld in the face of evil only at the price of believing what is unlikely to be true. It must confront evidential versions of the problem of evil.

# Chapter 6

# What's the Good of Free Will?

"Evidential" versions of the problem of evil are so-called because they allege that the evils of the world constitute strong evidence against theism, evidence that renders the truth of theism unlikely. The ambition here is more modest than that behind logical versions of the problem of evil, for the charge is not that the evils of the world render theism logically incoherent; rather, the charge is that it renders theism more likely to be false than true.

Now how is the theist to combat this charge? Well, she might do it along the same lines by which she responded to the logical version of the problem of evil; that is, by telling stories that—if true—would explain why God would allow the evils of the universe to take place. But she must also do something more. By leveling a more modest charge against theism, the advocate of the evidential version of the problem of evil has made the theist's task more challenging. No longer will it be acceptable for the theist to ignore the question of whether the story being told is plausible. Now, any story told in response to the evidential version of the problem of evil must have a case made for its plausibility, where the plausibility of a story refers to whether it is at least as likely to be true as it is to be false.

One such story, and a story that is crucial to responding to many versions of the evidential problem of evil, is none other than the free will defense that was developed in the preceding chapters. But because the emphasis there was simply upon showing that it is possible that moral evil is an inevitable but justifiable risk involved in the creation of free beings, a thorough attempt to defend the plausibility of this story was not undertaken. This is not to say that no attempt was made to establish the plausibility of the free will defense, for certain aspects of its plausibility were defended. I did argue, for instance, that science poses no obstacle to believing in libertarian freedom, that libertarianism makes better sense of moral responsibility than compatibilism and thus is a superior theory of freedom, and that the existence of freedom is the default position that has yet to be defeated. I did, that is, defend the plausibility of believing that human beings are free in a libertarian sense. I did not, however, consider one question that is crucial to the plausibility of the free will defense as an attempt to reconcile God's existence with moral evil. I made no significant attempt to defend the claim that free will is so great a good that God was justified in risking the torrent of evil that it has, in fact, given rise to. Thus it is that an advocate of an evidentialist version of the problem of evil might concede all the arguments given in the preceding chapters, but insist that the free will defense fails as an attempt to respond to evidentialist versions of the problem of evil for the simple reason that it is not plausible to believe that the value of free will is so significant as to justify the horrible things it has allowed human beings to do to each other, to themselves, and to other sentient beings. The point of this chapter is to show that this is not so and that it is, in fact, plausible to believe that freedom is such a great good that God was justified in bestowing it upon us despite the enormous risk involved. Before turning to my argument for this point, however, I will begin with an advisory of sorts.

## Of Proof and Probability

Do not enter the argument of this chapter with the expectation of finding a definitive demonstration of the claim that the value of freedom outweighs the disvalue of all the evils that are its responsibility. No such conclusive demonstration is forthcoming. Nor do I think that any is possible, and this for two reasons. First, I am not sure that any of us—even those who have suffered through horrendous individual torments—have anything like a sufficient grasp of the totality of evil that free will has introduced into the world. Nor, for that matter, is any individual that I know of particularly well equipped to make a similar judgment about the overall value of the goods that have been wrought by the free exercises of free creatures. Indeed, though I do not have the space to pursue it, I am fairly confident that the metaphors of calculation and weighing (can it seriously be thought that such language is not metaphorical and that a literal counting of valuable units is a possibility?) that are often used to discuss these matters are particularly inapt. This is not to say that I believe that such judgments of the relative worth or significance of values cannot be made, for I have no doubt that we make them frequently and accurately. It is only to say that such judgments have little to do with a counting up of values. Here it is instructive to reflect on the fact that most of us have a very clear idea of the kind of people in whose company we would like to find ourselves; nonetheless, I suspect most would also find it preposterous to suppose that this judgment is based on some kind of summation of numerically weighted values. It is likewise instructive to reflect on whether anyone has actually been helped in making a difficult decision by the following advice: Get some paper and a pencil, make a list of the pros and cons, and then see how the balance sheet plays out. Difficult decisions are difficult for sundry reasons that usually have nothing to do with adding up the pros and the cons. Sometimes the struggle is a moral one. Perhaps you are torn between self-interest—taking your dream job and moving your family across the country—and moral duty—refusing the job and remaining where you are so that you can stay close to your elderly, disabled mother whose greatest joy in life is to see her daughter and her grandchildren. Sometimes the struggle is an intellectual one. Assume that the city of the new job is an environment that would be much better for your children. How exactly does one decide whether the filial duty or the parental duty carries greater weight? However one does so, it is not, I submit, in any way that involves counting up value or adding up the pros and cons.[1] And if I am right in finding the quantitative model to be of little value in making value judgments about issues of comparatively limited scope, what hope can there be of using a quantitative approach in the kinds of global questions that must be asked in confronting the problem of evil?

Finally, it is important to note that even if one could calculate whether free will has been responsible for more good than evil, this calculation would still not settle the matter. We would still have to be able to make calculations about *(a)* the likelihood that the degree of evil in the world would follow from the production of free creatures and *(b)* at what level of likelihood would it become morally irresponsible for God to take the risk. Let us say the goodness wrought by freedom quantitatively outweighs the evil; however, there was, in fact, a 99.99 percent probability that a universe with free creatures would be an evaluative disaster; then we might justifiably complain that God acted irresponsibly in creating and simply got lucky. On the other hand, if the balance came out such that the total evil outweighed the total good wrought by freedom, but that there was only one chance in one billion that this would happen; then we might conclude that God had acted responsibly and was simply unlucky.

At any rate, these remarks about the practical impossibility of quantifying value are only to make the point that I will not in this chapter be trying to convince you that the total quantity of good inherent in and wrought by free will clearly outweighs the total quantity of evil that free creatures have wrought. I will only be attempting to show that free will is of such significant value that it is plausible to believe that its creation is worth the risk of the evil it has brought in its train. The same basic mind-set will apply in chapters 7 and 8, where my discussion of the evidential problem of evil will continue. In this respect my approach to evidential versions of the problem of evil is somewhat at odds with much of the current literature on the problem. Perhaps the most obvious respect in which my approach differs from others is evident from the frequency with which Bayes's theorem is made the centerpiece of treatments of the evidential version of the problem of evil. By contrast, Bayes's theorem will appear only once in this book—in note 2 for this chapter—and appears there only so you will know what it is I am eschewing.[2] It is not that I have any particular complaint against Bayes's theorem, nor do I think the literature in which it is deployed is without merit. Quite the contrary, I think much of it is insightful and rigorous; however, I find that almost none of the virtues of the literature that uses Bayes's theorem are a result of the use of the theorem. In my mind, all the interesting and vexing issues concerning the evidential problem that evil poses for theists are relevant to the initial probabilities that one would have to assign before one could even use Bayes's theorem. In addition, I am highly dubious about the possibility of assigning initial probabilities with even a modest confidence. The kinds of issues that one must grapple with in coming to terms with the evidentiary problem that evil poses for theism are the kinds of issues that the mathematics of probability seems particularly ill equipped to handle. When one is dealing with estimates of comparative value on a global scale, I do not have the least idea how one would go about making the kinds of probability assignments one would need to make in order to bring Bayes's theorem to bear. Consider the claim that whatever good God might produce via a miraculous intervention would be overshadowed by the evil of having a universe that is less than perfectly regular. Now, I know what it would mean to raise objections to this claim or to point to weaknesses in it or to allege that it is supported by other evaluative principles we accept; however, I have no idea of how to do this in such a way that the probability calculus could shed light on the proceedings. In the end, philosophizing about such matters involves telling stories and bringing reasons to bear and then stepping back and asking whether the story one has told seems plausible. That will be my approach, and I encourage you to probe, press, and pull apart the stories I will tell and then decide whether they seem on the whole more plausible than not. If fitting them into a Bayesian framework will help you do so, then by all means, calculate away. For my part, I shall be content to follow my hunches. You ought to do the same as you evaluate the arguments that follow.

## Freedoms Political and Metaphysical

It might seem a bit silly to devote a chapter to a discussion of the goodness of freedom. That freedom is a good thing, a good more valuable than life itself, will likely strike many readers as axiomatic and thus in need of no defense. But it is not prudent to entirely trust this initial reaction, if only for the reason that it may well result from a failure to distinguish between political freedom and metaphysical freedom. By political freedom, I have in mind freedom from tyranny and various other forms of governmental oppression; whereas, metaphysical freedom is that detailed in the first three chapters and amounts to an individual's ability to initiate conscious behavior for the sake of reasons. The two concepts are no doubt related in complex and significant ways; however, they are distinct, and we would be acting unfairly in defending the value of metaphysical freedom if we simply rested our case on the glow it acquires by basking in the light of approbation that is routinely cast upon political freedom by Western culture since the Enlightenment.

A case might be made for getting at the value of metaphysical freedom indirectly, by arguing that it is a condition for the possibility of political freedom and therefore is at least as valuable as political freedom. But this line of reasoning, it seems to me, either forges too strong a tie between political freedom and metaphysical freedom or it only succeeds in pushing the question back a step. On the one hand, it might be argued that political freedom is a good because it means that we will not be subjected to the frustration of our needs and desires that results from oppression. This, however, might equally be said of the oppression of brutes, without thereby committing ourselves to their freedom. The desires and needs that I frustrate by keeping a toad in a jar might all be part of a deterministic system; however, many—myself included—would find its suffering no less objectionable for that. On the other hand, one might argue that the real good of political freedom includes more than simply being free from having one's needs and desires frustrated. Political freedom is a great good because it respects the metaphysical freedom that human beings have to choose their own course in life. And this, of course, is where the question merely is pushed back a step, for we're here arguing that political freedom is a great good because it respects the great good that is metaphysical freedom. The following question is thus once more put squarely in front of us: What is our basis for believing metaphysical freedom to be such a great good that God's giving it to some creatures was a great gift?

Another reason that it is not satisfactory to simply defend metaphysical freedom via the value of political freedom is the following. As already noted, it is true that the vast majority of people would grant that being enslaved, in prison, or otherwise oppressed is bad, and being liberated from such a constraint is good. And one might even grant that the reason the former states are bad is because they frustrate our metaphysical freedom. But this alone is not sufficient to show that a universe with metaphysically free creatures is, ceteris paribus, better than one without free creatures, for one could explain our revulsion to oppression as contingent upon certain inclinations having been built into human nature. Yes, one might say, given that we are beings who seem to crave a high degree of autonomy, it is better that we be free from oppression so that we may thereby avoid the evil of frustration. But this no more means that it was a good thing that we were made to crave autonomy than our valuing shelter shows that it is a good thing that we are of such frail constitution.

Imagine someone waxing poetic about the value of hearth and home.[3] Now imagine that a person wants to argue—on the basis of the prevalence of such sentiments—that the human frailty that makes such a good of shelter is an intrinsic good and that the universe is simply better for having beings that need shelter than it would be if it lacked them. We would all, of course, recognize what was wrong with this defense of the intrinsic goodness of suffering. We would recognize that the goodness of shelter is tied in to the fact of human frailty and the desire for self-preservation. That we were made so frail as to need shelter to survive is certainly a fact about us, but it is far from clear that we are better for having been of such frail constitution. Human frailty, unlike freedom, is not something to which we generally attach value. But perhaps freedom is like frailty in that; perhaps it is a need that simply happens to be part of human nature, and our willingness to place such a high value on it stems from the fact that we suffer from intense frustration when this need is thwarted. But again, it does not follow from this that it is better that God made beings with this need than if there had been no such beings with the need. Now this is not to say that appeals to the value we place on liberation is of no use in establishing the goodness of freedom, for such appeals may still be relied on as evidence for the more general conclusion. It is to say, however, that the prevalence of such appels is not conclusive evidence for the intrinsic value of freedom, and one is well advised to proceed with caution when asserting the intrinsic goodness of some aspect of creation.

## Freedom and the Good of Moral Agency

Much was made in the first chapter about freedom of the will being a condition for the possibility of moral responsibility. Only if an action is freely undertaken does it make sense to either praise or blame the doer for the doing. Thus it is that a common and natural first step in explaining the value of free will is to note that without free will, there would be no moral agents. There would, in effect, be no morality or—at the very least—whatever moral principles there were would apply to nothing. Free will is, on this line, a great gift because it is only by having free will that we can be moral agents. But this is only the beginning of an answer, for it is reasonable to ask, "What's so valuable about moral agents?"

To answer this question, I will begin by contrasting two scenarios. In both, you are sitting in a musty attic sorting through the personal effects of your recently departed and much loved father when you make a discovery. In the first scenario you find your father's diary and discover that for the last twenty years of his life your father had suffered terribly as a result of developing multiple sclerosis. Gallantly, he had managed to hide the disease from his children and friends, not wanting them to be saddened or to treat him as especially fragile. In the second scenario, the discovery begins with your finding some boxes filled with pornography. At first you encounter your basic, dreary mass-distribution maga-zines—you know, ones with features on the women of various colleges—but the material you uncover grows progressively graphic and more disturbing. You find one box containing maga-zines of child pornography, but it is the final box that contains far and away the most disturbing material. In this box you find an infamous pornographic video. It is a snuff tape that was in the news a year or so ago when its producers were arrested as part of an FBI crackdown on pornography. But it is not simply that your father owned such a piece of smut; rather, the box is full of copies of the very same tape plus what appears to be a distribution list. Your father, it seems, was in the business of trafficking and hence profiting from pornography of the vilest sort.

Certainly neither of these discoveries is one that you would be pleased to make; however, there seems little doubt that most of us would much rather make the discovery described in the first sce-nario. Indeed, even if we do not suppose that the father was traf-ficking in the stuff in the second scenario and that he owned only a single copy of the snuff tape, I am still confident that the vast majority of us would much rather make the first discovery than the second.

The relevance of these contrasting scenarios to the present ques-tion is that our clarity about which discovery would be more dis-turbing illustrates a point that has been made by numerous philosophers. Socrates may well have been the first to make this point, and even if he is not the first, he is likely the philosopher who made it with more persistence than any other. The point is, simply, that nothing in human life—not even good health—is of greater value or importance than being virtuous. Awaiting an ex-ecution that seems likely to happen within two days, Socrates is approached by his friend Crito, who tries to convince Socrates to flee from prison. Crito has no doubt that Socrates' guards will readily accept bribes, and he urges Socrates to seize this last op-portunity to save his life. Socrates responds by reminding Crito that "the most important thing is not life, but the good life" and that "the good life, the beautiful life, and the just life are the same."

Thus it is that in deciding whether or not to escape, Socrates believes that there is one and only one issue to be decided.

> [T]he only valid consideration, as we were saying just now, is whether we should be acting rightly in giving money and gratitude to those who will lead me out of here, and ourselves helping with the escape, or whether in truth we shall do wrong in doing all this. If it appears that we shall be acting unjustly, then we have no need at all to take into account whether we shall have to die if we stay here and keep quiet, or suffer in another way, rather than do wrong.[4]

And some two thousand years later, German philosopher Immanuel Kant makes roughly the same point in what is certainly one of the most famous passages in all philosophical writing. It comes from his masterpiece on moral philosophy, *Grounding for the Metaphysics of Morals*.

> There is no possibility of thinking of anything at all in the world, or even out of it, which can be regarded as good without qualification, except a good will. Intelligence, wit, judgment, and whatever talents of the mind one might want to name are doubtless in many respects good and desirable, as are such qualities of temperament as courage, resolution, perseverance. But they can also become extremely bad and harmful if the will, which is to make use of these gifts of nature and which in its special constitution is called character, is not good. The same holds with gifts of fortune; power, riches, honor, even health, and that complete well-being and contentment with one's condition which is called happiness make for pride and often hereby even arrogance, unless there is a good will to correct their influence on the mind and herewith also to rectify the whole principle of action and make it universally conformable to its end. The sight of a being who is not graced by any touch of a pure and good will but who yet enjoys an uninterrupted prosperity can never delight a rational and impartial spectator. Thus a good will seems to constitute the indispensable condition of being even worthy of happiness.[5]

For Kant and Socrates, the best that can become of us is that we become beings of good will. Wealth, health, fame, intelligence—these are all fine, but they pale in comparison with living a morally good life.

Now I cannot at present do all that I should to defend this point. I could not do so without turning this into a work on ethics. Nonetheless, it seems to me that this is a point that most people would accept and, moreover, even if they wouldn't, I am happy to go on record as maintaining that they should. It seems to me as close to an axiom in ethics as one is likely to find. In my estimation, it may well be the least controversial of all the claims that I make in this book.

Its relevance to the question of what is valuable about freedom runs through the fact noted previously: Free will is a necessary condition for a being having the status of a moral agent and is thus a necessary condition for there being virtuous individuals. Without free beings the universe would be deprived of that which may well be its greatest source of value: people of good will. And if the universe cannot have what may well be its greatest asset without beings of free will, then that is a very powerful justification for God's having created such beings despite the risks attendant thereto. Indeed, this might be deemed a decisive reason were it not for the fact that the Socratic principle seems to provide as equally compelling a condemnation of free will as it does a reason for valuing it so highly.

The argument thus far, an objector might note, focuses on only one half of the Socratic principle, the half that maintains that a person of good moral character is a most valuable thing. But, it might be observed, the other side of the principle is equally in play here. That's the side that says that a morally corrupt person is a most disvaluable thing. And just as free will is a necessary condition for there being people of good moral character, so it is equally a necessary condition for there being people of depraved moral character. Thus it is that free will can be praised as a condition for the possibility of there being people of good will, but can also be bemoaned as a condition for the possibility of that most catastrophic of human disasters, a person of corrupt moral character. The value that attaches to free will in virtue of its role in there being people of good will seems to be counterbalanced by the disvalue that attaches to free will in virtue of its role in there being people of evil will. Thus it is that the significance of free will as a source of moral worth would appear to be a standoff, with the great good of the virtuous counterbalanced by the great evil of the vicious.

I do think it is possible to break this deadlock and break it in favor of the value of free will; however, before indicating how I believe this can be done, it may be well to offer a few comments about how it should not be done. First, it would not be satisfactory to observe that we have no way of knowing that the numbers of free beings who become corrupt is equal to or even likely equal to the numbers of beings who will stay the path of righteousness. It would not be a satisfactory response because the objection does not depend upon knowing that in fact there are exactly as many free beings who become corrupt as those who stay the path of righteousness. Nor does the objection necessarily suppose that the total value of the entire pool of free agents is a straightforward tally of the total numbers on either side of the divide. The objection depends only upon recognizing that a lost soul is as great a catastrophe as a saved soul is a blessing. As I did not base my argument for the goodness of free will on anything like an additive function, the objector certainly need not do so. Second, it would be beside the point to observe that the evil wrought by free beings—to themselves, in this case—is their responsibility and not God's and that we would therefore be wrong to blame God for their corruption. It would be beside the point because here the issue is not whom we should blame for the evil that already existent free beings do; rather, the issue is whether the risk inherent in creating free beings that some of those beings would become moral disasters is a risk that it was reasonable for God to take. That the risk becomes reality is the responsibility of the free beings that fail, but that there is the risk at all is God's responsibility. And when we evaluate whether God's taking this risk was reasonable, we must attend to the potential evils of the risk as well as its potential benefits. The objection here is merely indicating that we have no good reason to suspect in this case that the chance of the benefits is of greater significance than the risk of the problems.

While neither of these responses to the objection is satisfactory, the second points the way to a more promising answer. That corrupt free beings have become so of their own free wills is relevant to the way in which this deadlock can be broken, though not relevant in the way just suggested. To see how it is that the culpability of evil beings is relevant to this issue depends upon recognizing that another significant good of our world is the good of justice being done. When evil people do evil deeds, it is good that they receive appropriate punishment. This is not to say that it is good that there is evil so that there is occasion for justice being served, for it would, of course, be better still that none go the way of corruption. It is only to say that the disvalue of the situation is partially mitigated by the fact that an appropriate punishment is meted out. And this is enough to show that the great value of the free development of just souls is not directly nullified by the catastrophic disvalue of the free development of unjust souls, because the depth of disvalue inherent in a corrupt person is mitigated by the good inherent in justice being done.

Now this might seem a puzzling way to break the apparent deadlock between the value of the virtuous and the disvalue of the vicious, for one of the standard versions of the problem of evil points to the fact that the righteous suffer and the wicked often flourish. There is, it would seem, no correlation between one's welfare and one's moral character. But the puzzlement here can easily be dispelled by noting that the justice that is to break the deadlock is justice that will be done in an afterlife and not in this life. Thus it is that the apparent indifference to the demands of justice exhibited by our world is not the end of the story. Nor is it illicit to appeal to an afterlife at this point in the debate, for what we are trying to establish is that it is plausible to believe that an omnipotent, omniscient, and omnibenevolent God might judge that free will is such a great good that it was justifiable for Him to decide to create free beings despite the degree and quantity of evil that would result thereby. And when we are discussing what it is reasonable for God to decide to do, we must certainly take God's omnipotence seriously, as God undoubtedly would. To exclude considerations pertaining to the afterlife is to act as if what God can do through his omnipotence is not relevant to God's decision of what to create.[6]

Now having suggested this way of breaking the deadlock, I must confess that the case presented thus far for the goodness of free will seems rather marginal. I should feel a good bit better if an additional reason could be given for assigning free will such a vaunted status in the hierarchy of goods. Fortunately, I believe that there is additional reason, a reason that is found in the good of love relationships.

## Love and Free Will

Imagine that a drug, we'll call it La Flèche,[7] has been developed and that the effect of the drug is such that any person to whom it is administered will immediately fall hopelessly in love with the first person they see. I know that by beginning thus I am aligning myself with a long list of mediocre movies and TV shows in which one of the protagonists devises and deploys—with madcap results!—some love-inducing potion or spell or machine or mantra. In defense of my using this device, I plead no less a precedent than *A Midsummer's Night Dream*. At any rate, imagine that such a drug is available and that you decide to administer it to Tiger Mussels, the guy of your dreams. But unlike the sitcoms mentioned earlier, there is no madcap result. He doesn't fixate on a census taker who happens to appear at your door at the precise moment the drug is taking effect; rather, he suddenly becomes completely devoted to you, loves everything about you, and cannot spend enough time with you, while, of course, being respectful of your space.

Now, we might well find such an act to be a despicable violation of another's autonomy, but let us set that aside for now. What I want to discuss is the fact that—irrespective of the moral transgression involved—we feel that Tiger Mussels's attachment to you is a cheap imitation of real commitment and real love. Nor do we think this is a marginal call, in the way that we might think of a cultivated pearl as being of somewhat less value than a natural pearl, while still being roughly the same kind of thing. No, it seems to me that we tend to view the chemically induced commitment as being a fundamentally different kind of thing, and a thing of dramatically less value than love that is not so induced.

In attempting to explain why this should be so, it is natural to say things like "the man had no choice in the matter" or "he was forced to love" or "he did not enter into the relationship freely." And what this suggests is that a necessary condition for the possibility of one being loving another is that the former being is free.[8] And what this further means is that a defense of the value of freedom can be made on the basis of the fact that it is a condition for the possibility of that which is among the most prized of human conditions, being able to love and be loved in return.

To further convince yourself that it is the absence of freedom that is relevant to our judgment that the chemically induced love is not real, it is worth noting that we would take it to be meaningful to wonder whether that "love" could, over time, turn into the genuine article. That such a question is not dismissed as meaningless is significant for two reasons. First, it presupposes that the initial chemically induced state is not real love. But second, the chance that the induced "love" might turn into the genuine article over time can lead one to ask what would have to change about the situation for it to count as real love. Certainly nothing about the man's behavior or feelings would need to change, for it was stipulated that they were all exactly as they would be if he really loved her. The only component lacking from the situation that would lead us to say that the love is not real is that the man did not freely choose to be in the relationship that he is in. And what it would mean for the man to really come to love the woman would be for him to have the freedom to leave and yet freely decide to stay, and stay for reasons of love.[9]

Lest the basic point of this thought experiment be misunderstood, a clarification is in order. The present suggestion is not that one can simply to choose to fall in and out of love in the way that one can choose to turn on or off the TV. Falling in love is surely a more complicated state than such a caricature would suggest. What is being maintained, however, is that a crucial condition of being in love is that one be a free being. To see that there is a legitimate role for freedom to play in love relationships, it is important to distinguish between love and having the kind of strong feelings that we generally associate with love relationships. One might, for instance, have longful feelings for a person and yet not have a love relationship insofar as one does not give in to or act on those feelings. It is in this latter respect that freedom becomes an essential ingredient in a love relationship; it includes an element of freely chosen commitment. Thus it is that being in love is a much more complex state than simply being disposed to have what I have called the "longful" emotions. Nonetheless, it seems to me a widely shared intuition that a necessary condition for the authenticity of a person's love is that the love be entered into freely.[10] And if this is so, then we have a very powerful reason for thinking freedom a great gift. Without it, no love would there be.

Now even if one grants that libertarian freedom is a necessary condition for the possibility of meaningful human relationships, one might still wonder why God could not have secured the possibility of such goods without giving us the freedom to do as much harm as we can actually do. The opponent of theism can still ask, What is the benefit of human beings having the capacity to inflict such significant harms on one another and on other sentient beings? Or, to put the matter from the side of those victimized by others, Why did God make us as vulnerable as we are to the wickedness of others? In the next section I will present two possible replies to this question. First, I will defend the view that vulnerability is a condition for the possibility of love relationships. Second, I will argue that the significance of one's moral successes is directly related to the degree of what is at stake in one's actions; that is, the greater the significance of that which is placed in one's trust, the more it is to one's credit if one faithfully cares for that with which one was entrusted.

## Love and Vulnerability

Though my focus in the preceding section was on showing that free will is a necessary requirement for there being a real love relationship, I do not want to suggest that freedom and what I there called the longful feelings are the only essential components to being in a real love relationship. At the very least, I would want to add that a commitment to promote the welfare of the beloved is another essential ingredient in a love relationship. So it is that one might say that an abusive husband has longful feelings and freely chooses to stay in the relationship, but does not really love his wife in that he is not committed to her welfare. And once this is recognized, it is natural to concede that a certain measure of vulnerability of the beloved is also required, for a commitment to promote the welfare of another implies that the other's welfare might be frustrated. And where the welfare of another might be frustrated, there is a certain measure of vulnerability. Thus it is that a case can be made that genuine love presupposes the vulnerability of the beloved.

Some, I imagine, will think this a confusion. It is true, it might be said, that loving a being who is vulnerable does require a commitment to that being's welfare, but it does not follow from this that a being must be vulnerable in order to be loved. In fact, any theist who buys into the aforementioned connection between a being's lovability and its vulnerability is going to run into serious problems when the requirement that one love God is considered. On the principle concerning the connection between love and vulnerability, one will have foreclosed on the possibility of loving God, for God is the epitome of an invulnerable being.

This objection, however, rests on a false assumption. What it assumes is that the only kinds of vulnerabilities that one can have are vulnerabilities with respect to one's own existence or individual welfare. Ask any parent whether this is so, however, and you will likely get an argument. Most parents can conceive of no greater misfortune befalling them than to have their children suffer some great misfortune. For a parent, the most significant vulnerabilities they have are grounded in the vulnerabilities of their children. And if it is right to think of God's love for us as being somewhat analogous to the love of parents for their children, then it certainly seems plausible to suppose that God's act of creating beings who are under His care is a source of significant vulnerability to God. And for Christians, this point also emphasizes the significance of the Incarnation; that is, God's becoming man in the person of Jesus Christ in order to suffer for the sins of humanity.

Nor is this a circular defense of the connection between vulnerability and love, for there is no problem in God's loving us, for we clearly are vulnerable. But once there is a basis for God's loving us, then there is a basis for God's being vulnerable insofar as our sufferings wound our loving Creator. This, however, is only a partial reply to the objection that love is only conditionally connected to vulnerability. While it explains how a metaphysically invulnerable being might still have other vulnerabilities, it does not respond to the suggestion that the connection between love and vulnerability is conditional. It does not explain, that is, why God could not have created creatures who could love one another and Him without there being any vulnerabilities. The response to this part of the objection, however, should now be evident from the fact that freedom is a necessary condition for a love relationship and the fact that there are vulnerabilities other than one's physical welfare. Given that freedom implies the possibility of spurning another's love, and given that freedom is a condition for the possibility of loving, it follows that God could not create loving beings who would not be vulnerable in a moral, emotional, and spiritual sense. Thus it is that it is at least plausible to believe that there could be no love in a world without vulnerabilities.

Now while this helps explain why it is important that we have some vulnerabilities, it does not explain why these vulnerabilities are as significant as they are. Perhaps it explains why there must be the chance of some harm awaiting each of us, but it does not explain why some of these harms are allowed to be so extreme. It does not address the problem of moral atrocities.

## Unanswerable Atrocities

The heading for this section reflects more where I shall wind up then where I shall begin. For I shall begin by offering an answer to the question of why we have the capacity to do horrible things to one another, including those among us who are most vulnerable and innocent. It is a sad commentary on the frequency with which children are victimized that I need not mention any specific cases. Every reader, I am sure, will be able to supply a case with which he or she is familiar and would be easily up to the task of illustrating the fact that there are cases of moral evil that seem far in excess of what is required for love to be possible or freedom deemed significant. There is, however, one point that has not yet been discussed but that does have relevance to such moral atrocities. It is the fact that the significance of one's acting responsibly is in direct proportion to the value of that which was placed in one's care. Thus it is that perhaps the greatest moral achievement of any human being's life is to have taken good care of the weakest in their midst. If children were made so as to be largely impervious to the acts of adults, then it would never be to an adult's credit that a child was well cared for.

Now while this seems to me true, it also strikes me as a pale justification for the kind of suffering that some children have endured. In the end, I do think that the horrendous suffering that their fellow humans visit on children is suffering for which I, at least, am unable to come up with any sufficient and plausible explanation. Thus it is that though I think the points just made are relevant to the issue of explaining why God would allow horrendous moral evil, I also believe that they are woefully inadequate. Though I will have more to say about such moral atrocities later and will bring up other factors that are relevant to explaining why God might allow such monstrous deeds, I will conclude here with a concession to the advocate of the evidential argument from evil. Even anticipating those stories I will tell in future chapters, I am unable to come up with any plausible story as to why God would allow such deeds to occur.

I end this chapter, then, by conceding that there are evils for which I can tell no plausible theistic story. And having admitted this, I also note that matters are about to become much more difficult for the theist. Already a concession has been made that there are what Augustine called "untraceable evils," and we have yet to consider at any length the special problem posed by natural evil, a problem to which the free will defense seems—at least on the surface—irrelevant. It is to this problem that we now must turn.

# Chapter 7

# Natural Evils

Witnessing a flood of the Musketaquid River inspired Thoreau to compose an ode to its beauty. "The river swelleth more and more," he began "Like some sweet influence stealing o'er." And after twenty-six lines of intervening but similarly adulatory verse, Thoreau concludes with the following meditation:

> Methinks 'twas in this school of art
> Venice and Naples learned their part,
> But still their mistress, to my mind,
> Her young disciples leaves behind.

Now it would be folly to disparage the inspiration behind these pleasing lines, for nature can be a source of exquisite beauty. Still, such lines do prod the impulse to sarcasm when it is remembered that on August 1, 1976, this same mistress spawned a flash flood in Colorado's Big Thompson Canyon that killed 139 campers and hikers who had been lured to the spot by nature's great beauty. It is hard not to wonder whether it was perhaps Thoreau, and not the landscape, that was being stolen over by some sweet influence. It is hard not to extend to Thoreau the same patronizing concern that he extended "To a Stray Fowl" when he muses that "I fear imprisonment has dulled thy wit, / Or ingrained servitude extinguished it." And though I have no desire to dispute Thoreau's suggestion that the beauty of work wrought by human artists and artisans is hard-pressed to rival the grandeur that nature can manifest, the need for balance demands that we also note that the horrors nature visits upon us give us reason to wonder whether human savagery can rival that manifested by the natural order. Now given how bad human beings can be to one another, you might be tempted to write this last claim off as too extravagant, and you might be right to do so. Before doing so, however, you ought to consult a medical dictionary and look up Lesch-Nyhan syndrome. Here, nature's art has made human beings who have a compulsive tendency to self-mutilation. As soon as a Lesch-Nyhan baby's teeth grow, those teeth must be pulled; otherwise the baby will begin to eat away its lips and fingers and any other part of its body that can reach its mouth.

## Natural Evil and the Free Will Defense

It is a striking fact that as cruel as human beings can be to one another, nature seems up to the challenge of rivaling the cruelty of its free inhabitants. It is also a fact that poses a serious obstacle to the attempt to show that the evils of the world do not render belief in God unreasonable. It does so because it opens up the theist to the following objection: While we might exonerate God for the moral evil in the universe by insisting that the only way such evil could have been prevented would have been for God to deprive human beings of the great good of human freedom, this strategy has no immediate application to the problem posed by natural evil. For an answer to that problem, the theist must, it would seem, look elsewhere.

Now in one sense, this seems to me perfectly true. It is true in the sense that the precise strategy of the free will defense cannot be applied successfully to the problem of natural evil. This does not mean, however, that human freedom has no role to play in reconciling natural evil with God's existence. Quite the contrary, I believe it has a fairly significant role to play, for as we will see shortly, one standard way of answering the challenge posed by natural evil does very quickly bring us back to the issue of the value of freedom.

The standard strategy I have in mind here can be summarized in the following three claims: *(a)* there are sound reasons for believing that it was good for God to have created a natural order; *(b)* having a natural order entails that nature behave in an orderly way, namely, it conforms to natural laws; and *(c)* that when free beings are put into a system of nature that operates according to nearly exceptionless laws, it is inevitable that they are sometimes going to get caught in the gears of the mechanism that is nature.[1]

Now this strategy obviously cries out for further defense. As a starting point, one might begin by wondering why it is good that there be a natural order. Or, to put the matter another way, one might justifiably wonder why it is important that the environment in which we find ourselves be lawlike.

## Nature's Order and Human Action

It is sometimes alleged that it is important that human beings live in an environment that exhibits regularities because in the absence of such an orderly environment it would not be possible for human beings to be free in any meaningful sense.[2] Sure, I might still choose to pull the trigger on a gun, but if this action were to be undertaken in an environment in which there were no natural laws, then the action would not have the moral significance that it has in our world. In the absence of an ordered environment, one would have as much reason to believe that pulling the trigger would be followed by the sprouting of daisies from the gun's barrel as one would have to believe that the result would be the propulsion of a hardened projectile at a lethal rate of speed. And the same would go, of course, for actions that we normally think of as virtuous. The box of candy that you leave at the door of a neighbor might suddenly explode and spew flaming shards about the neighborhood. If *anything* were to go in nature, then there would be no reason to *do* anything, for the consequences of one's doings would be utterly unpredictable. Divorced from their orderly consequences, actions would no longer have the moral significance that they now have. Thus it is that an ordered natural environment is necessary for the possibility of human beings engaging in morally significant actions. And the possibility of engaging in morally significant actions is one of the central reasons that free will is valuable. Therefore, having free will in a meaningful sense seems to require that there be an ordered environment in which to act. And thus it is that the free will defense may be of some help in explaining natural evil. It can explain why the environment in which we conduct our affairs must be an ordered one.

## A World of Sound and Fury

Some readers will have undoubtedly noticed that there is a sense in which the examples above are not coherent. The incoherence is found in the fact that if our environment suffered from the kind of massive irregularity presupposed by the examples, then it is far from clear that we would have the kinds of objects—guns, daisies, candy, explosives, fire—involved. But far from being an indictment against the theist's contention that there is value in having an ordered environment, what this incoherence highlights is that there is an even deeper reason that it be important that our environment be ordered. This deeper reason is the following: In the absence of order, it is not clear that it is possible to have an environment at all. It is only because things have relatively stable properties that we can identify them as things at all, and it is only because we can identify them as things that we can classify them as belonging to certain kinds and as having certain natures, natures that ground their tendencies to behave in specific ways under specific circumstances. In a radically irregular environment, it would not make sense to talk of a gun that variously sprayed bullets or daisies or water. It would not make sense for the simple reason that there could not be guns or bullets or daisies in a radically irregular realm.

And it is not unreasonable to push this point even further and wonder whether it would make sense to think of there being reality at all in the absence of order. To get a sense for why this might be so, consider why we take it for granted that waking experience is more real than dreamed experience. Is it not because the experiences we have while awake are more regular and stable? that they constitute more of an ordered system than the experiences we have while dreaming?[3] And if this is right—as I believe—then it seems that regularity and stability are criteria that we use for marking the real off from the unreal. And if that is true, then it seems that we would not have good reason to take a disordered environment to be real. Now one might say that there would still be a reality in the absence of order, for what we now call illusion would be our reality, and thus the illusory would be elevated to the status of the real. There may be something to this objection; however, it seems to me that it would be more accurate to describe matters in precisely the reverse fashion; that is, what we would have would not be an elevation of the illusory to the current status of reality but rather a downgrading of the real to the level of what is currently illusory.[4]

Thus, even though it may be going too far to suggest that the presence of order is a condition for the possibility of there being anything whatsoever, it is not too much to suggest that it is a condition for the possibility of there being reality in the robust sense that we currently encounter. And if it is a condition on the possibility of there being reality in our robust sense, then it seems that there is a very important reason that nature need be ordered. The very universe in which we live and move and breathe seems to depend upon it.

## Between Order and Evil

It is easy to imagine, however, that even if an atheist were thus convinced that order is indispensable to our having a real environment in which morally significant choices are a possibility, he may be little moved by this consideration. The most obvious problem with this explanation of natural evil, he might say, is that the requirement that there be an order does not demand that the order have the potential to inflict harm. Why, the atheist can justifiably ask, couldn't nature have been made of softer, or we of sterner stuff?

One way of answering this question and the way that will constitute a significant portion of my own reply is that an order with edges can contribute to the spiritual and moral welfare of the order's free inhabitants. There are, in fact, several distinct ways in which this reply has been fashioned in theistic apologetics. Perhaps the two most noteworthy ways in which this response has been developed and the ones that I shall focus on herein are the accounts by

Saint Augustine and Saint Irenaeus. I do not, however, offer these as two components of a coordinated defense. Indeed, I could not even if I wanted to, for the accounts disagree in several crucial respects. Nor is it my purpose here to defend one of these theodicies against the other, though my sympathies are ultimately on Augustine's side. I offer them because it seems to me that either view is a perfectly respectable account of why God might have created a natural order that is other than uniformly benign.

## Of Pain and Pinocchio

I must confess to having no great love for many children's classics. I am even guilty of what amounts to blasphemy in philosophical circles: I have little appreciation for Lewis Carroll's *Alice's Adventures in Wonderland*. I found it opaque and disturbing as a child, and as an adult I find it, well, opaque and disturbing. I have no plans to inflict it on my own children. Though it was not as opaque, I found *The Adventure of Pinocchio* rather disturbing as well. For one thing, the world in which I grew up was not as menacing as Pinocchio's. For another, the punishments visited upon the wooden one seemed far out of proportion to his crimes. Of course it was nice in the end when he saved Geppetto's life and became a real boy, but this seemed almost like an afterthought. I bring this up not because I am so deluded as to think anyone is interested in my cranky opinions about children's literature. I bring it up because I have come to a greater appreciation of the story of Pinocchio since reading John Hick's defense of an Irenaean theodicy in *Evil and a God of Love*. Perhaps I should explain.

A side of the story that I paid little attention to as a child was that the fairy was able to give Pinocchio life at the outset; however, she was unable to make him a real boy. This was something that she was able to do only at the end of the story. Now as a child, I always understood his becoming a real boy as a kind of reward that the fairy withheld until Pinocchio had earned it by eventually choosing to walk the path of virtue. But perhaps it is more accurate to say that the fairy was not able to make Pinocchio a real boy from the outset. Perhaps his becoming a "real" boy could happen only through the kind of growth that a free being undergoes by confronting and overcoming temptation.[5] Perhaps even a magical fairy cannot bestow moral character with the stroke of a wand. Perhaps it takes a course of self-creation by a free being to achieve moral maturity. That this is so should really not be all that surprising, especially if we can trust the arguments given earlier in defense of libertarian freedom. After all, if being free is a condition for moral responsibility, and if developing a character that is morally sound is largely a product of the free choices that one actually makes, then it would seem to follow that being a person of moral maturity is not something that can be conferred magically on one by a second party.[6]

That moral maturity is not something that can be bestowed on one by a second party is a fundamental tenet of Irenaean theodicies. Human beings, it was suggested by Saint Irenaeus in the second century A.D., were created as works in progress, the completion of which was left to the human beings themselves. The incomplete works produced by God are free beings who are as yet morally and spiritually undeveloped. Their moral and spiritual characters they must forge, like Marley's chain in *A Christmas Carol*, through the free choices they daily make. And this was not done by God simply because he thought it would be good for the creatures to help out or have something to do. God created human beings in an incomplete state because even omnipotence cannot directly create a being of moral and spiritual maturity. It is, after all, the case that being a person of moral and spiritual worth is to one's credit. And one's character can be to one's credit only if it is the product of one's free choices. Thus it is that God could no more directly create morally and spiritually mature beings than God could directly create "free" beings whose "free" choices he would cause to be on the side of virtue. A character to one's credit can no more be directly caused by another than can a free choice that is to one's credit.

Now what all this has to do with nature's crueler edges becomes apparent when we get more specific about what constitutes moral and spiritual maturity. The kinds of traits that we prize include courage and compassion, perseverance and patience, fidelity and fortitude. But these are all traits that it would be hard to imagine developing in the absence of vulnerability. Thus it is that the development of free beings of laudatory character could take place only in an environment to which those free beings were vulnerable. And thus it is, according to Saint Irenaeus and John Hick, that the presence of a harsh environment is an important ingredient in God's setting the stage for the emergence of beings that could enter into relationships of genuine love and friendship with Him and with one another.

## Spiritual and Moral Redemption

Though it also stresses the beneficial effects that suffering can have on one's spiritual and moral development and growth, Augustine's theodicy is in one way the inverse of Irenaeus's account. For Augustine, human beings were created as fully formed free beings who then fell to a lesser state of perfection as a result of original sin, the sin of loving themselves before God. The story of humanity is, for Augustine, not so much the story of beings who are in a process of development as it is the story of lost souls who must find their way home. In the Augustinian story, nature's harshness serves as a reminder that this world, the material world, is not our true home, not our ultimate source of fulfillment and perfection. That fulfillment can only be found in God, a point that Augustine expresses with characteristic eloquence. "Our hearts are restless until they rest in you, O Lord."[7]

Now it might here be alleged that the Augustinian story is fundamentally incoherent. If this world does not fulfill us and if our hearts are restless until they rest in God, then what need is there for nature to beat the stuffings out of us as well? The mere fact that nothing can satisfy us as God can should be enough motivation for us to turn to God.

What this criticism overlooks however, is the fact that finding one's way home, turning one's life over to God, is a painful and difficult exercise according to Augustine. It involves no smaller a task than desisting from placing oneself at the center of the universe. And the simple fact is that given the choice between the difficult (yet ultimately more fulfilling) and the easy (yet less fulfilling), human beings routinely choose the path of ease. Separated by original sin from our true source of fulfillment, we fumble through one attempt after another to quiet the longing and desperation that plague our souls. Augustine seems to me right in deeming this restlessness to be part of our nature. But it also seems to be a fact about our constitution that we can settle for an unsatisfying torpor provided that there is nothing too threatening or painful looming over us. Having become separated from God, there is a danger that we might despair and settle for what is not our true home. I have spent afternoons watching hour after hour of television, fully aware that I was creating a history that was more a vacuum than a life. It was a pleasant distraction, but almost as soon as it was past, there was nothing of substance to look back upon. And yet, I did it, fully knowing that I was embracing far less than I might. I did it because it was easy. I did it to avoid the frustration and effort attendant to shouldering a true challenge or worthwhile goal. God does not want us to resign ourselves to the limited goods of this world, and nature's harsher edges are one way of preventing us from settling.[8]

## Coldhearted Calculations

Though it is hard to dispute its initial plausibility, some have found the view that God allows natural evils for the moral and spiritual development or reformation of his free creatures to have untenable implications. In critiquing the position of C. S. Lewis, who may well be the best-known contemporary advocate of an Augustinian theodicy, John Beversluis makes the following observations:

> Some people who do not suffer seem far from God while others who do suffer seem close to him. There are flourishing atheists and terminally ill believers. Yet if we accept Lewis's argument, we must con-

clude that those who suffer only appear to be close to God but in fact are not—otherwise why do they suffer? We must also conclude that those who do not suffer only appear to have drifted from God but in fact have not. Furthermore, the more you suffer, the further from God you are; and the less you suffer the closer you are.[9]

Beversluis finds such conclusions both untenable and reprehensible. They are untenable because they do not match our experience of the distribution of happiness and suffering in the world. They are reprehensible because they involve telling someone who suffers horribly—as a result of cancer perhaps—that his suffering is his own fault, for it is visited upon him only because he is a spiritual slacker. And I would have to agree with Beversluis here in terms of his contention that such conclusions are both implausible and reprehensible; however, it seems to me that neither Lewis nor Hick need be saddled with them. There are several reasons that this is so. The first is that neither Hick nor Lewis believes that pain is the only instrument by which God can call human beings back to himself. Thus, when confronted with a suffering individual, we are not allowed to conclude that the individual is further from God than a non-sufferer. The simple fact may be that suffering is the most effective means of redemption or development in the one case and not the other.

Another reason that Lewis and Hick need not be troubled by Beversluis's critique is that they accept the notion of stages of spiritual development. Supposing that spiritual development allows for different levels of maturity, it is possible that an individual whose spirituality is highly developed might still suffer, since suffering is the most effective means of moving that individual to the next stage and thus even closer to God. That we are all, even the best among us, in need of further spiritual improvement is found, for instance, in Lewis's suggestion that "when the saints say that they—even they—are vile, they are recording truth with scientific accuracy."[10]

A third reason that the Beversluis's criticism does not work is that it is open to Lewis and Hick to contend that some suffering may be for the benefit of a person other than the one undergoing the suffering. It is with this in mind that Lewis notes that part of the good that can result from suffering is "the compassion . . . and the acts of mercy" that it can elicit from those around the sufferer.[11]

But perhaps the most important point to make in response to the charge that the Augustinian and Irenaean theodicies have cold-hearted implications is the following: The criticisms assume that natural evil plays its transformative role with a sensitivity to specific cases. Nothing, however, in either the Irenaean or Augustinian theodicies demand that this be so. This is important for the simple reason that in the case of some natural evils, it is highly implausible to believe that the evil wrought on each individual is doing some specific spiritual or moral work on that individual. When you have 100,000 wiped out in a typhoon, it is not plausible to believe that each death wrought by the event was directed to the end of spiritual or moral transformation or both. To be at all plausible in the face of disasters of such enormity, the Irenaean and Augustinian theodicies should be understood only as asserting that the natural order is a kind of medium that can have value for the ends of soul-making and soul-reformation. A natural order with harsh edges can play this role in a general sense and without sensitivity to the specific spiritual and moral state of those who run afoul of its harsher edges. Indeed, such indifference to the specific spiritual needs of specific individuals is precisely what one would expect when one mixed an ordered nature with free beings. Nonetheless, even though specific natural evils are not targeted for specific individuals, those natural evils can still have a salutary spiritual and moral effect for those who are open to growth or redemption. And this same response can be extended to the cases of the suffering of infants and animals. Neither infants nor animals are in a position to benefit spiritually from the suffering inflicted by natural evils; however, if the foregoing analysis is correct, then it is open to the theist to say that the suffering of infants and animals is a regrettable by-product of having a natural order that is harsh enough to play the transformative role it was designed to play.

But even if the suggestion that salutary natural suffering can be inflicted by an order that is indifferent to the nuances of individual cases does adequately answer Beversluis's objection in one stroke, it does not enable Augustinian and Irenaean theodicies to answer all the concerns that are raised for the theist by the specific natural evils that are part of our world. In the next section I explain why I take this to be so and why the theist, thus, has more work to do.

## Inscrutable Natural Evils

As was the case with the defense of the value of free will given in the preceding chapter, the kind of response to the problem of natural evil given in this chapter works fairly well as long as one moves on a rather abstract level. When, however, one is forced to look at specific cases of horrendous natural evil, it becomes much more difficult to make out a plausible case.

The atheist, for instance, might grant that an ordered nature is important, but still proceed to wonder why God, if there is a God, does not intervene periodically to prevent nature's more savage manifestations. Perhaps there must be an order, even an order with severe edges, but would it really undermine the goods of orderliness for God to prevent, say, the deaths associated with the Sanriku tsunami described in the Introduction. Let it be granted that reality requires a high degree of regularity. There does not seem to be any like requirement that the regularity be absolute. Moreover, it is not even clear that God could prevent nature's more horrifying episodes only by violating nature's regularity. Given that libertarian free choices are not necessitated by prior events in the natural order, there would seem to be nothing in violation of the natural order were God to intervene in times of dire need by implanting certain choices into his free creatures. God could, for instance, have caused all the residents of Kamaishi and Yoshihama to decide to hike several miles inland in the hours before the sea would rise to claim them. This would, of course, have involved a compromise of the freedom of the town's inhabitants; however, it is not clear that it would have been a morally significant compromise. It would have prevented certain virtuous and vicious deeds from taking place; however, once the tsunami had passed, the

people could have been returned to their own wills and then proceeded to visit on one another most of the same blessings and
blights that would have been their work in the hours before the
disaster.

Now I can think of stories that one might be tempted to tell
here. One might, for instance, contend that communal tragedy
contributes to the good that is a sense of communal responsibility.
Such communal disasters illustrate dramatically what John Donne
reminds us in verse; that is, "No man is an island." While I think
there is something to such an explanation, I have to admit that it
leaves me largely unmoved. The kind of communal disasters that
occur seem far in excess of what's needed to reinforce the value of
community. Did the great influenza epidemic of the early twentieth century really need to claim several million lives to reveal that
we should not ask for whom the bell tolls? Far less would have
seemed to me sufficient.

Another story one might be tempted to tell is that there are some
long-term goods that are served by disasters of such enormous
scope. If the end result of allowing the great influenza epidemic
was a genetic culling of the human species that contributed to,
say, 10,000 additional generations of human beings that would
not otherwise be, then perhaps it would be reasonable for God to
allow it. The problem with such a story, however, is that I can give
absolutely no reason for thinking that it is so. It might be a handy
story to tell concerning the logical version of the problem of natural evil; however, it is not much use when the standard for a successful response is plausibility and not just consistency.

And the atheist also need not rest his entire case here on disasters of such wide scope. He might instead puzzle over especially
horrifying natural evils. He might point to something like Lesch-
Nyhan syndrome. The most vile human being would be hard-
pressed to come up with something as awful as Lesch-Nyhan
syndrome, so why does God permit it? Are there worse natural
disorders in any other nature that God might have created? It is
hard to see why this would be the case. Would God's preventing
all cases of Lesch-Nyhan through miraculous intervention impose

too great an irregularity on the natural order? Well, Lesch-Nyhan is not that common a syndrome. How irregular would nature have to be to prevent its occurrence? And if the regularity of nature is the overriding concern, why couldn't God see to it that couples who would be genetically disposed to beget a Lesch-Nyhan baby occasionally make choices such that they do not meet or, if they do meet, they do not engage in sexual activity. Surely it cannot be made out that God's planting the relevant choices in such individuals would significantly compromise their freedom. They would still be free to engage in all the other free activities in which human beings routinely engage.

Thus it is that I conclude this chapter on the same note that I concluded the preceding chapter. I am forced to concede that there are some evils, in this case natural, for which I can tell no plausible story as to why God would allow them. In the next chapter, I consider whether the fact that there are such inscrutable evils does demand that a theist concede that at least some of the evil in the universe renders belief in God irrational.

## Chapter Eight

# Inscrutable Evil

You and your spouse have been invited to a friend's house for dinner. On the drive there, your spouse insists that you missed the turn to the friend's house; however, you are convinced that you are still on the right road and that the real turn to your friend's house is five miles ahead. Well, five miles come and go, as do ten and then twenty. Meanwhile, your spouse is growing increasingly adamant that you should turn around. "We've clearly missed the turn," comes the grousing. "It only takes thirty minutes to get from South Milwaukee to Janet Rascal's home in Racine. We've been on the road for over an hour now." Undaunted, you continue to drive on, convinced that the correct turn will appear at any minute even as it is pointed out that "it was thirty miles ago that you said the turn was just another five miles. I know because I checked the odometer when you made that brilliant proclamation." Now one thing you might do under these circumstances is cling to your belief that you had not missed the road. "No" you would insist, "maybe the odometer is malfunctioning. I think I remember reading about how untrustworthy they are. And as for the time, well, perhaps our watches are both running far too fast. Oh, and that 'Welcome to Illinois' sign—well that's probably some high-schooler's prank. Kids, why I can remember when I was on the high school drill team and we took a pickled salmon and stuffed it with fried cheese curds and then crammed it into Edgar's tuba. . ." Yes, you might stick to your guns in such a case. But clearly the reasonable thing to do would be to admit that you were wrong, that you had made a mistake and then turn around. For this is a case where one of your beliefs—that is, you did not miss the turn—runs into so many recalcitrant facts that it is no longer reasonable to cling to it. (By a recalcitrant fact, I mean a fact for which there is no plausible explanation consistent with your original belief.

All the plausible explanations for a recalcitrant fact would involve the rejection of your original belief.)

Now in the last chapter, a concession was made to the advocate of the evidentialist version of the problem of evil. It was there admitted that there are some cases of evil that amount to facts that are recalcitrant to theism; that is, some evils such that there are no plausible explanations for their occurrence where those explanations would be consistent with believing in a God who is all-good, all-powerful, and all-knowing. The question to be addressed in this chapter is whether the existence of recalcitrant evils forces the theist to admit that the only reasonable course is to stop and turn around, by either rejecting theism entirely or by qualifying one or more of God's attributes. I will argue that they are not, and that inscrutable evils—recalcitrant though they be—do not have the force of making the theist's persistence nothing more than an irrational stubbornness.

## When Recalcitrant Facts Aren't

One of the most heartrending aspects of the Mann Gulch fire of 1949 is the story of the third survivor. You have already heard the story of Rumsey and Sallee's flight to safety, but no mention was made of how a third man escaped with his life. On that day, as the thirteen smoke jumpers were beginning their race from the blowup, their leader—a man named Dodge—did something inexplicable. Out in front of his men he stopped, knelt down, and lit another fire, a fire that began to consume the dry brush in front of him. Because of Dodge, whose job it was to direct and look out for the smoke jumpers under his charge, the plight of those very smoke jumpers seemed to have been compounded. In addition to the fire pursuing Dodge's men, they now, thanks to him, had a fire in front of them and around which they'd have to navigate to escape from the blowup that was rapidly closing. Sallee remembers well his puzzlement over Dodge's behavior. "I saw him bend over and light a fire with a match. I thought, 'With the fire almost on our back, what the hell is the boss doing lighting another fire in front of

us?'" What the hell, indeed. The dry brush at Dodge's feet crack-
led and then blazed. Soon it was an impressive fire in its own
right. Granted, it was no blowup, but in a matter of seconds it was
substantial enough that, as Sallee recalls it, the men thought their
boss "must have gone nuts," when he walked into the center of the
burning patch he had just ignited and began motioning and calling
for them to do the same. The men, who either couldn't fathom
their leader's actions or did fathom his plan but didn't believe it
would work, would have none of it. Dodge recalls matters thus:

> After walking around to the north side of the fire I started as an avenue
> of escape, I heard someone comment with these words, "To hell with
> that, I'm getting out of here!" and for all my hollering, I could not
> direct anyone into the burned area. I then walked through the flames
> toward the head of the fire into the inside and continued to holler at
> everyone who went by, but all failed to heed my instructions; and
> within seconds after the last man had passed, the main fire hit the area
> I was in.

And as soon as they made their decision not to follow Dodge's
lead, all the men but Rumsey and Sallee sealed their fate. All that
was left for Dodge was to lie down in the smoldering ash of his
escape fire and wait as the blowup passed around him.

We can easily understand why Dodge's men did not follow his
lead. Dodge's coming up with something as outrageous as an escape fire under the circumstances was a moment of stunning clarity in the midst of catastrophic conditions. Dodge calculated that
he and the majority of his men would never make the top of the
ridge. Their only option was to create an oasis of embers in which
to take refuge, and that is exactly what Dodge did. But the men
either did not understand their boss's plan or simply did not believe that lying down in the middle of a fire was a better plan than
trusting their twenty-year-old legs. Except for Rumsey and Sallee,
they all judged wrongly, for there seems no reason to suppose that
the men would not have survived if they had only followed their
leader's directions. We can, of course, see why they didn't follow
their boss. In their training no mention had ever been made of

lighting an escape fire. Indeed, even Dodge did not recall having been schooled to take such action. "It just seemed," he would later recall, "the logical thing to do." His men, tragically, did not see the logic.[1]

It would, of course, be absurd to fault Dodge's crew for not following his lead. With only seconds in which to make a decision, they couldn't be expected to both comprehend and assess his plan; nonetheless, Dodge's ill-fated attempt to save his men does illustrate the fact that our inability to come up with a satisfactory explanation of another's behavior does not always mean that it is plausible to believe that there is none. And this is especially true if the behavior is that of one whose knowledge and experience is greater than one's own. If Dodge's men had only trusted their boss's knowledge and cool head instead of their legs, they may well have all survived.

So it is that the Mann Gulch tragedy intersects our discussion of the problem of evil at yet another point. Where the difference in knowledge and experience between Dodge and his men was significant by human standards, it is utterly insignificant when compared to the difference between human understanding and divine. And if it can happen that one human being can sometimes fail to fathom the reasonableness of another's behavior because they lack the latter's wisdom, we should count it as highly likely that there are reasons available to an omniscient being of which we have utterly no comprehension. And if this is so, as careful as we should be in concluding that a Dodge in our life has no good reason for what he is doing simply because we can see no good reason, we should be extremely slow to conclude that God can have no reason for allowing some state of affairs simply because we can see no reason. Thus it is that cases of inscrutable evil do not necessarily make it clear that the theist should reverse course. We have good reason to believe that there are reasons for many of God's actions that we simply cannot grasp.[2] In what follows, I will discuss two respects in which God might have reasons that are simply beyond the grasp of human cognitive powers. I will call the first of these moral modesty, and the second modal modesty. The basic idea behind both is that God's knowledge of moral and modal issues so outstrips ours that it is not reasonable to infer that there is no reason for one of God's actions simply because we are aware of no reason that would justify God's permitting the state of affairs in question. Indeed, once we take seriously the suggestion that God's is all-knowing, what would truly be surprising is if none of God's doings were puzzling to us. If you were reading a bit of science fiction about an alien of vastly greater intelligence than any human being, you would not give the story high marks for plausibility if all of the alien's actions were easily comprehended by the intellectually inferior earthlings. What you would expect in such a story is that some of the alien's behavior would be incomprehensible to human beings. And why should our expectations be any different with respect to a being of supreme wisdom? Looked at in this way, far from being troubled by inscrutable facts, theism would seem to positively predict that such facts there would be. And surely we cannot fault theism if one of the things it would lead us to expect turns out to be the case.

## Moral Modesty

Near the beginning of the summer of 1975, when I was fourteen, my brother Mark and I discussed the possibility of driving out to Colorado in order to go backpacking in the Rocky Mountains. A few weeks later his interest in the plan began to waver. He had just graduated from high school, and his high school sweetheart was scheduled to be away for most of the summer. As bad luck would have it, the only chance they would have to spend time together was during the two weeks in which we had our window of opportunity to go camping. After that they would be parting again to attend different colleges. And so it was that there was to be no backpacking trip in the summer of 1975. I could see that the trip was no rival for my brother's interest in spending time with his girlfriend, but I could not appreciate the weighting of values that led him to make this decision. The reason, of course, was that romance—at that time—registered only very faintly on my evaluative radar. It was not that I was still at an age where it was utterly valueless; however, I still could not understand how spending time with one's girlfriend could possibly compete with a weeklong adventure in the mountains of Colorado. On the one hand there were evenings in which we would open our brotherly hearts under starstrewn skies and days of filling our lungs with the thin mountain air and of discovering hidden pools in high mountain streams that were thick with native trout; perhaps we would even see a bear in our excursion. On the other hand there was, well, spending time with one's sweetheart, an activity that I could appreciate wanting to devote an evening to provided there was not much else to do, but two weeks? When the trout and the bears and the stars lost out in my brother's decision, the conclusion he had reached was one that I was largely at a loss to understand.

Now, the point of the story is not that my brother's decision was the correct one. In fact, given that he later fell in love with and married an entirely different woman, a woman of whom I wholeheartedly approve, I think it manifestly clear that he made the wrong decision at the time. (I have yet to forgive him for it.) Nonetheless, having fallen in love and gotten married myself in the interim, I now have to concede that I have come to appreciate the value of romantic love in a way that was beyond me at the age of fourteen.

What this bit of autobiography illustrates is that our moral or evaluative perspectives are capable of maturing, and part of the process of maturation is coming to recognize either entirely new values—things of value that had never occurred to one or had never occurred to one as being valuable—or values that one was already aware of but had accorded far too little or far too much weight. I have little doubt that as I get older, I will encounter yet more cases of what might be called normative epiphanies, cases in which a new value enters my moral horizon or a value already recognized undergoes either a dramatic increase or decrease in significance. Indeed, I feel so confident that this should be the case, that if it does not happen, I will take it to reflect not that there are no more normative epiphanies to be had; rather, I will take it as evidence that I have failed to make significant progress in wisdom on matters moral.

Now it is important to note what underwrites this conviction that increased wisdom and experience ought to be accompanied by an expanding of one's moral horizon. What underwrites our confidence in this regard is two things: *(a)* most of us have experienced normative epiphanies as we have matured, and *(b)* as beings with finite and highly imperfect minds, it would be silly to believe that we had reached a point in our understanding of values such that we had the complete story and had it down to such a degree that there was nothing significant left to learn. So if it is reasonable to conclude that we do not have a perfect grasp on the full range or proper prioritization of values at any point in our lives, then it is equally reasonable to expect that as long as we continue to grow in wisdom, we will continue to grow in our knowledge of the nature of values.

But if this is true, then it seems all the more reasonable to conclude that there must be values recognized by God of which human beings have no understanding. Given that the disparity between the understanding of the wisest human being and God is vastly greater than the disparity that would obtain between any two points in the development of a human being's life, anyone who accepts the foregoing claim about the reasonableness of expecting normative epiphanies as we mature should be even more strongly committed to the reasonableness of believing that there are goods that God must reckon that have never occurred to the human heart. And this, of course, is one reason why an evil's being inscrutable to us is not sufficient grounds for concluding that God would not have a sufficient reason for having allowed the evil in question.

But moral modesty is not the only reason that we should be reluctant to conclude that a state of affairs for which we can see no reason is a state of affairs for which God can see no reason. There is at least one other reason we ought to be slow to draw such conclusions.

## Modal Modesty

A modal claim is a claim about whether something is possible or impossible, necessary or contingent. Philosophers have long been in the habit of taking the constraints upon the human powers of imagination and conception as revealing modal truths. So, for instance, it might be said that if we can conceive of something or imagine something consistently, then it follows that the state of affairs being conceived or imagined is possible. On the other hand, it would also be held that if our attempts to imagine something involves a contradiction so that we really cannot conceive of or imagine it, this means that the state of affairs we are trying to imagine is impossible. Finally, if our attempts to imagine or conceive of something not being the case leads to a contradiction, this would mean that the thing we are imagining or conceiving must, of necessity, exist.

There are at least two reasons that one might want to question this procedure. First, one might question its reliability in principle. For example, one might argue that we have no good reason for thinking that what can be established in thought is a reliable guide to what can be in reality. If one were to go this route, one might be willing to say the following: *(a)* it is true that a square-circle is a contradictory thought that cannot be coherently conceived, and *(b)* there might really be square circles. If one did this, then one would have very good reason to be modest about our modal intuitions and one would, consequently, also have good reason not to take cases of inscrutable evil as evidence against God's existence for the simple reason that our ability to consistently conceive of God as eliminating a certain evil in no way indicates that it is really possible for God to do so. Having said this, however, I must observe that I have no desire to question whether something that was clearly inconsistent in thought might really be possible. If we cannot rely on our well-formed modal intuitions, then it is unclear upon what we can rely in identifying modal truths.

One might, however, concede the reliability in principle of the use of our powers of conception for identifying modal truths, but then proceed to question the reliability of the procedure as it is actually put into practice. Here, one would grant, for instance, that the ability to conceive a state of affairs without contradiction is a reliable touchstone for identifying possible states of affairs, but then one would proceed to complain that the claim to have conceived of something consistently is often made with troubling haste. It is from this standpoint that I wish to cast doubt on many of our modal intuitions.

In chapter 7 it was observed that one might wonder why God had not made human infants so as to be impervious to the onslaughts of both nature and other human beings. Here we might imagine babies floating peacefully belly up on the surface of any water into which they happen to fall and hard objects being reduced to fluff when they encounter the baby's tender skin. All germs, moreover, would wither and die before they could penetrate a baby's immune system. It seems, in short, easy enough to tell a story about invulnerable babies that is logically consistent— a consistency that is revealed by our ability to imagine "invulnerable" babies. Unlike the case of a square circle discussed in the Introduction, there is really no problem to our giving content to the state of affairs that would correspond to there being invulnerable babies.

Now it seems to me that this last claim is true: We can give content to the supposition of invulnerable babies by imagining something that looks very much like a human baby and yet is impervious in the ways described. However, this should not be taken as conclusive evidence that there could be such invulnerable human babies, and this for the simple reason that there may well be reasons buried in human nature or the connection of human beings to their histories that make the supposition of real human babies that are invulnerable an incoherent notion. To insist that there is nothing inconsistent about the supposition, we'd have to have a clear and complete grasp of that which constitutes the essence of a human being. When we're talking about the impossibility of a square circle, it seems reasonable enough to claim that we grasp the nature of squareness and circularity in enough depth to see that they are really inconsistent. Or when we are talking about whether we could reverse the order of the cards in a deck, we have experience enough of their having been in different orders that we have good evidence to believe it is possible. But what, on the other hand, is supposed to ground our confidence that there could be invulnerable human babies. Unlike the varying order of cards in a deck, we have never experienced the state of affairs to which we now refer. And to trust our judgment merely on the basis of the fact that we can imagine it to be so is really too hasty. Here are some of the questions I should want answered before I could conclude that there could be invulnerable human babies. At what age would the babies cease being vulnerable? At what age would the babies begin to be able to inflict harm on others? Is having once been utterly dependent on others an essential trait of adult human beings? How would the attitudes of human parents to their babies differ if those babies were invulnerable? Is an invulnerable being an appropriate object of love?[3] And if not, could a being be a baby without it being an appropriate object of love? I, for one, do not have the first idea of how to answer such questions. And even if I did, I suspect that I would still wonder whether being vulnerable is part of what it is to be a baby.

Now one might counter this line of reasoning by supposing that God might have bypassed the period of infancy entirely. God might have simply had human beings spring, fully formed, from seed pods and thereby bypassed the vulnerability of infancy. But here too, we must wonder whether it is clear that human beings could have been begotten otherwise than by biological procreation by other human beings. Moreover, the need for moral modesty here reemerges, for it can well be asked whether it is obvious that a world in which there were no babies and hence no atrocities inflicted upon them would be superior to the actual world. I, for one, find nothing obvious about it. I am certainly comfortable calling specific states of affairs good and others evil, but when it comes to assessing the value of a world that would differ from ours in such a wholesale way, I am largely at a loss about what to say. This is not to say that I have no confidence about the goodness or evil of fairly large-scale changes. For instance, I take it to be a good thing that polio has been largely wiped out in civilized society and think it would be good to wipe out cancer and HIV. I do, however, contend that such "large-scale" changes are still of an order of magnitude far less than that involved in a situation in which there would be no human infants. In addition, it is reasonable to maintain that a world without infants would lack significant value by not having infants and that this lack of value would not be paralleled in a world without the HIV virus.

It would, however, be impossible for me to give a general critique of the modal intuitions behind all such suggestions as to how God might have structured the universe so as to eliminate inscrutable evil; nonetheless, I do think I have done enough to show that one should be suspicious of any such account that seems to move swiftly over what are actually very complex issues of value and modality, especially where the account runs through our powers of imagination.

## Avoiding Moral Skepticism

There is, however, a danger involved in the theist's riding modal and moral modesty too hard. The danger is that it may force the theist to eventually wind up in a position of moral skepticism. When I see you suffering through some difficulty that I have the power to alleviate, should I not be reluctant to intervene for fear that I might disrupt some important good that God was pursuing in allowing the evil to occur. If I have no good reason to conclude that such is not the case, then it would seem that I have just as much reason to intervene as I do to stay out of the situation and let God do His work.

Imagine that a person you know well has fallen into a life of dissipation and dissolution and that despite your repeated attempts to help him, he only continues to sink further in his ways. Realizing that your "help" has only served to prop him up, you decide that the best thing for him is to cut him off, let him hit rock bottom, and then hope that the shock of falling so far will cause him to shake off his corruption. There is, you well see, no guarantee that this will happen; however, you have correctly estimated the situation in judging that it stands the best and perhaps only chance of success. Now having adopted this course, you would find it troublesome if some acquaintance begins—perhaps out of sympathy—to prop this person up in precisely the way that you discovered to be so destructive. It is with good reason that you would be irritated. Perhaps you would not fault the other person for the damage done, for they did not know all that you do about the dispositions of your corrupt friend; nonetheless, the fact would remain that a person acting out of ignorance would have thwarted the sound plan of action that you had adopted. It would have been better had the stranger not interfered. This scenario is relevant to the viability of moral and modal modesty in that the epistemic modesty advocated therein might lead one to worry that we, as creatures, might be doing precisely this sort of damage whenever we meddle in the sufferings of others, for we may well be interfering with divinely laid plans that are grounded in reasons that are hidden from us.

The concern that modal and moral modesty pose for the theist is thus the following: If the foregoing contention that we have no reason to suppose that God might not be allowing some evils for reasons beyond our ken is sound, then it would seem to be equally plausible to suppose that the occurrence of any evil is such that God might be allowing it for reasons beyond our ken. But if that is so, then it would seem to follow that for any instance of evil that we could prevent, we have as much reason to allow it as we do to prevent it. After all, if we have as much reason to believe that the evil is being allowed for some reason beyond our ken as we do to believe that it would be better for the evil to be prevented, then we would seem to have no more reason to intervene when we can do so than we would to refrain from intervening.

The flaw in this reasoning is that it is perfectly consistent to believe the following propositions: *(a)* God gave human beings a moral law to follow because that set of laws would be a reliable guide to human action and would enable human beings to most efficiently contribute to God's overall plan, and *(b)* God's overall plan for the welfare of the universe and its inhabitants involves factors of which human beings have no awareness. So it might be the case that God allows some evils to occur for reasons beyond our ken and that it is right for us to always prevent evil when we can do so without forfeiting some greater good of which we know. Our acting, that is, on a set of moral rules that God has revealed to us may be part of God's plan for promoting some more comprehensive set of values of which we have only a partial picture.

But even though moral and modal modesty do not entail that human beings should refrain from promoting their conception of the good, it might still be thought to impose a general skepticism concerning the ultimate nature of the good. An atheist might, for instance, reason as follows: The implications of moral and modal modesty as here developed do demand a complete rewriting of our system of values, for nothing short of such a complete abandonment of what we hold dear could possibly underwrite the kinds of horrendous things that happen to children at the hands of nature and humanity. Whether one is talking about a brutal molestation and murder of a child or the case of a child afflicted with Lesch-Nyhan syndrome, the situation is the same. Such is the depth of some cases of horrendous suffering that we have good reason to believe that there is no good—known or unknown—that could possibly justify their occurrence. And thus it is that the suggestion that God might have reasons for allowing such horrendous suffering, where these reasons are beyond our ken, ultimately does demand an abandonment of our set of values. It does so because it demands that we abandon the bedrock moral belief that there is nothing—known or unknown—that is worth the price of the horrendous suffering of innocent children. And if it is the case that the moral and modal modesty defended in this chapter imply that God's values might be wholly other, what meaning is left to the theist's contention that God is all-good? At best, it seems to reduce to the contention that God values what God values, whatever that might turn out to be. And what legitimate reason could there be to follow, let alone worship, a being so opposed to human standards of value? Any decent and rational being who was invited to partake of whatever "values" would justify such horrendous evils should, respectfully, return the ticket.

This last phrase I have borrowed from the character Ivan in Dostoyevsky's *The Brothers Karamazov*. But this is only fitting, for Ivan's speech in *The Brothers Karamazov* may well be the most powerful version of the objection I have just stated. It is to Ivan's challenge that I turn in the next chapter.

## Chapter Nine

# Horrendous Evils and the Good of Procreation

Though Ivan's speech in *The Brothers Karamazov* is frequently cited as a classic statement of the challenge evil poses to theism, a central feature of this challenge has been largely neglected in philosophical treatments of the problem of evil. The challenge that I have in mind is posed in the following passage, a passage in which Ivan pushes Alyosha to confront the question of whether any goods could possibly counterbalance the horrendous suffering of a five-year-old child that has been savagely tortured by its parents.

> Imagine that you are creating a fabric of human destiny with the object of making men happy in the end, giving them peace and rest at last, but that it was essential and inevitable to torture to death only one tiny creature—that baby beating its breast with its fist, for instance—and to found that edifice on its unavenged tears, would you consent to be the architect on those conditions? Tell me, and tell the truth.[1]

While the majority of philosophers' attempts to respond to the problem of evil have focused on identifying reasons why God might not be able to produce a universe without evil or on reasons why we are simply not in an epistemic position to make judgments about the kinds of constraints that might limit even an omnipotent being, little attention has been paid to Ivan's central charge: Such theodicies and defenses are utterly incapable of dealing with the horrendous suffering of that five-year-old girl for the simple reason that there is no good that could justifiably be purchased at the price of such suffering. Ivan's suggestion is, quite simply, that there is no need to list goods that might be purchased at such a price and that there is no need to speculate about why God might be limited in bringing about those goods, for there is nothing that would be worth the price of that child's misery. Given the choice between *(a)* creating a world that was perfect in all other respects (including respects we cannot fathom) and yet contained this one instance of horrendous evil and *(b)* not creating at all, our moral intuitions tell us that God ought not to have created at all. That this challenge has been comparatively neglected is especially surprising given the fact that the task of developing theodicies and defenses only makes sense if this prior challenge can be met.

One philosopher who appreciates the full force of Ivan's charge is Marilyn McCord Adams. In "Horrendous Evils and the Goodness of God" she uses it as an occasion to reflect on the impotence of most theodicies and defenses to deal adequately with the problem of horrendous evil.

> In the spirit of Ivan Karamazov, I am convinced that the depth of horrific evil cannot be accurately estimated without recognizing it to be incommensurate with any package of merely non-transcendent goods and so unable to be balanced off, much less defeated, thereby.[2]

This is not to say that Adams ultimately sides with Ivan and his posture of rebellion against the Creator; rather, it underscores her conviction that a satisfactory response to the problem of evil must appeal to the transcendent values of the Christian faith in order to make sense of God's creation of a universe that allows for horrendous evil. It is for a want of such appeal to uniquely Christian values, according to Adams, that the vast majority of theodicies and defenses are not equipped to handle the threat posed by horrendous evils. She concludes that "it is not only legitimate, but, given horrendous evils, necessary for Christians to dip into their richer store of valuables to exhibit the consistency of" the existence of horrendous evil and the existence of a God who is all-knowing, all-powerful, and all-good.[3] In the course of her essay, Adams gives eloquent expression to several such valuables crucial to overcoming the challenge posed to theism by horrendous evil. One of these is a communion with God made possible because one's own horrendous suffering allows one to identify with the suffering of Jesus Christ. Thus it is that Professor Adams's position is very much in line with Alyosha's. Ivan's devout younger brother concedes that he would not be the architect of paradise at the price of the five-year-old's suffering, but then proceeds to note that there is a Being that can overcome the challenge of horrendous evil, a Being that "can forgive everything, all and for all, because He gave His innocent blood for all and everything. You have forgotten Him, and on Him is built the edifice, and it is to Him they cry aloud, 'Thou art just, O Lord, for thy ways are revealed.'"[4]

My purpose in this chapter, however, is not to question the validity, force, or significance of Adams's various attempts to use Christian valuables to illustrate how horrendous suffering might be engulfed or defeated by God. Quite the contrary, I find her work in this direction to be both valid and of great significance. What I do dispute, however, is the contention that traditional theodicies and defenses making no appeal to soteriology and other uniquely Christian concerns are incapable of rising to Ivan's challenge.[5]

The competency of traditional theodicies to handle horrendous evil is challenged by Adams in two main respects: *(a)* their focus on global goodness (the value of creation considered as a whole) is at odds with the Christian belief that God has love and goodwill for each human being (what I will call the thesis of divine universal benevolence) and *(b)* their attempt to balance off horrendous evils with religion-neutral values fails to recognize the depth of horrendous evils; a depth so profound that horrendous evils are incommensurate with and so cannot be balanced off by any distribution or quantity of merely immanent goods.

In the first section of this chapter I will focus upon the aforementioned distinction, arguing that God's love for individual human beings is consistent with his allowing the individuals to suffer from horrendous evil. In the second section I will question the validity of the moral intuition behind Adams's position, arguing that if this intuition were correct, then we would likewise be committed to the moral wrongness of procreating the human species.

To forestall certain misunderstandings of the arguments to follow, some preliminary remarks are in order. First, it is no part of this chapter to show that it is plausible to believe that there may be modal constraints upon God's creation of the world, modal constraints that, for all we know, may have made it logically impossible for God to create a world as good or better than the actual world but devoid of evil. The challenge posed by Ivan and Adams is a prior challenge, maintaining that such constraints are irrelevant to the problem of horrendous evil insofar as there are no goods of this world that could engulf let alone defeat horrendous human evil. Second, I will be using the terms "balance off" and "defeat" in the senses developed by Chisholm, where balancing off is a simple additive function and defeat defines a more complex relationship in which the defeated evil is part of a whole, the value of which would be diminished if the evil were to be removed.[6] Third, though I recognize Alvin Plantinga's distinction between a theodicy and a defense, it is not a distinction crucial to the argument that follows.[7] Thus it is that I will use the terms as loose synonyms to avoid the ungainly practice of always using some sort of disjunctive construction. Finally, it is worth noting that the challenge posed by horrendous evil may well be narrower on Adams's construal than it is on Ivan's. Where she maintains only that horrific evil is incommensurate with any package of non-transcendent goods, Ivan's challenge seems to be that horrendous evil is incommensurate with any package of goods, immanent and transcendent. In this essay I will be focusing upon the challenge as formulated by Adams; however, it is worth noting that a solution to her version of the challenge would equally solve Ivan's. If horrendous evil can be shown to be balanced off by the class of immanent goods, then it surely can be balanced off or defeated by the class of immanent *and* transcendent goods.

## Divine Love and Wretched Lives

Horrendous evils, according to Adams, are evils that provide prima facie reason to doubt that the one experiencing the evil (either as sufferer or perpetrator) has a life that is good on the whole.[8] It is important to note that the reason to doubt the overall goodness of a life plagued by horrendous evil is only a prima facie reason. Her dispute with traditional theodicies is not about whether horrendous evil can be engulfed or defeated; rather, it is about the range of goods that must be in play for engulfment or defeat to even be possible.

The core of Adams's complaint about traditional theodicies emerges from a distinction and a moral intuition. The distinction is that between two challenges posed by the existence of horrendous evil: *(a)* the challenge of reconciling God's goodness and love for the universe, given the state of creation taken as a whole and *(b)* the challenge of reconciling God's goodness and love for individual human beings, given the states of their individual lives taken as wholes. In making this distinction, says Adams, one is in a position to see that the global and religion-neutral goods routinely used to respond to the first challenge are unable to meet the second challenge. Thus it is that while she thinks religion-neutral theodicies may be able to rise to the first challenge, the fact of horrendous human suffering renders them utterly ineffectual in dealing with the second problem.[9]

God cannot be said to be good or loving to any created persons the positive meaning of whose lives He allows to be engulfed in and/or defeated by evils—that is, individuals within whose lives horrendous evils remain undefeated.[10]

But this seems to me to not be so. One can consistently adhere to the goodness and love of God with respect to some individual the goodness of whose life is engulfed or defeated by horrendous evil. Surely a parent who is powerless to prevent the horrendous suffering of a child does not thereby have her goodwill or love of the child called into question. Moreover, we also would not impugn the love and goodness of the parents if they were able to prevent the child's suffering and yet were unwilling to do so because doing so entailed bringing about an even greater evil than the child's suffering. It is, it seems to me, not true that loving an individual or having goodwill with respect to an individual entails that one accord the individual's welfare absolute priority in one's scheme of values. And this seems right even if we stipulate that the love is perfect. A perfect love ought to be commensurate with the value of the beloved, and if the value of the beloved does not trump all other values, a perfect love would not treat it as if it did.

And it is not to the point to reply that the parent—unlike God—is not omnipotent, for the stipulation at the outset was that there may be modal constraints upon God's creation of an order with free creatures that we are simply unable to grasp. Nor is it correct to suggest that the parent—unlike God—was not responsible for creating this being, for many cases of bringing forth a new human life are entered into both freely and with the knowledge that the child being born is entering a situation where there is a real possibility of horrendous evil.

Thus far, all I have argued is that it is consistent with God's love and goodness with respect to an individual that the individual's life be engulfed or defeated by horrendous evil. I have not, however, shown that it is plausible to believe that horrendous evil can be engulfed or defeated by some set of merely immanent goods. It is to this task that I now turn.

## Horrendous Evils and Human Goods

To understand how one might respond to Adams's contention that no quantity of immanent goods is sufficient to balance off horrendous evil, it is important to note that it—much like Ivan's challenge—relies heavily on an appeal to our moral intuitions about the profundity of horrendous evil. It trades on our intuitive recognition of the fact that the horrendous suffering of human beings and especially children is a price that no amount of immanent good can justify. A story in the news as I write this chapter details the case of a mother who tossed her eighteen-month-old son from a car moving in excess of seventy miles per hour. Such cases incline us to believe that if we were given the choice—in effect, God's choice—to create a world in which we knew that such atrocities would occur or to not create at all, the morally correct option would be to not create at all.

But there is reason to doubt whether our moral intuitions about the depth of horrific evil actually support the conclusion that God ought not to have created at all even if this were the only alternative to creating a realm with horrendous evil. The reason is found in the fact that the same principle renders it morally insupportable for human beings to have further children. That some percentage of the children brought forth in a given year will suffer horrendous evil is, it seems to me, an exceedingly well-supported inductive generalization. To be sure, the percentage might well be reduced if human beings entered into procreation only under very favorable conditions; however, it is equally clear that some children conceived under very favorable circumstances will still suffer horrendous evil. What this means is that the only way, at least for the foreseeable future, to bring an end to cases of horrendous suffering would be to have human beings refrain from procreating altogether. Now, setting aside the practical impossibility of bringing about such a moratorium on reproducing, I assume that we do not think that we would be morally obliged to achieve such an outcome. And I do not think our moral intuitions here can be sufficiently explained in terms of concerns over violating the rights of individual human beings to reproduce, for our moral intuitions are equally mute about the prospect of undertaking a noncoercive campaign to convince others not to reproduce. Even if worldwide voluntary celibacy were a real possibility, our intuitions tell us that we would be under no moral obligation to promote it.

Thus it is far from clear that the goods of this world alone would not be up to the task of justifying God's decision to create even in the face of horrendous evil. And thus it is that God's willingness to create our universe while recognizing that it will most likely contain instances of horrendous suffering does not demand an abandonment of our current set of values. Indeed, if the contentions of this chapter are correct, our willingness to bring new lives into the world despite the fact that some of these lives will be horrendous shows that we do not believe that there is no reason that would justify the creation of an order that includes horrendous suffering. By procreating, we participate in the maintenance of such an order and we think it morally unobjectionable to do so. It is, according to our scheme of values, a horrendous price to pay; but a price that is nonetheless worth paying to perpetuate the existence of free creatures like ourselves.

*Chapter Ten*

# Belief Beyond Evil

I began this book by noting that the problem of evil can be seen as the charge that theists are guilty of a kind of intellectual myopia. Theists cling to belief in God's existence only by turning a blind eye to the scope, depth, and variety of the world's ills. In this, the last chapter, I'd like to suggest that there is a different sort of myopia that one must guard against in working through the problem of evil. This myopia is born of the fact that evil stands at center stage in attempts to solve the problem that it poses for theism. It is, of course, fitting that this should be so, for it would be a sorry exercise to set out to solve the problem of evil and not attempt to tie one's theories and arguments back to the evil that is the root of the problem. But that it is fitting that evil should assume the spotlight in discussions of the problem of evil makes it no less a source of potential intellectual blindness.

## The Good, the Bad, and the Hideous

One way that working on the problem of evil can be a source of intellectual blindness is that it can lead one to start thinking of evil as the dominant theme in the world's history. Given the lavish illustration that the world's troubled history provides for the problem of evil, it is easy to start taking it as a surd fact that the world is, on balance, a very bad place. The problem with this conclusion, however, is that it is far from an obvious fact, surd or otherwise, that the world is as bad as all that. There is, after all, much in the world to cause one to sing the glory of its creator if such a creator there is. This, in a way, is one of the morals that can be taken from the preceding chapter. If the world is as unrelentingly and dominantly horrible as it can seem when one has an eye primarily on its ills, then it is the height either of ignorance or of twisted self-gratification that human beings would view the birth of an infant as an occasion for joy. This too is why I might justly be thought to have been unfair in the sarcasm I directed against Thoreau's verse at the beginning of chapter 7. To fail to acknowledge the depth of the world's evils is a kind of intellectual myopia, but it is no less myopic to treat the world's goods as of obviously lesser moment. Against those who wax a touch too romantic about nature's wholesomeness, a favorite example is that of the ichneumonid wasp. This delicate winged creature captures some other insect, which she then converts into a live incubator for her eggs. Once those eggs hatch, the larvae proceed to feed on their captive but still living host, a host that is kept alive for some time despite being eaten because the clever little larvae save the life-sustaining organs for last and thereby ensure the continued freshness of their feast.[1] But while the ichneumonid has its place in exposing the fatuousness of viewing nature as a gentle and nurturing mistress, it is no less fatuous to take the ichneumonid as revealing the hidden underbelly that is the true essence behind the patina of nature's softer golden hues. For all nature's potential to inflict hardship on humans and for all its bizarre and cruel and repulsive manifestations, when we are forced to make an all-things-considered judgment on its value, our verdict seems clear and immediate—the natural environment is of great value. And before you dismiss this as a judgment we are never really inclined to make, ask yourself why you are deeply disturbed at the news that we are losing in the neighborhood of 30,000 species of plants and animals each year.[2] Yes, the world is bad, but given the choice to have it continue as it is or have it end, utterly and irretrievably, most of us would choose its continuance and feel confident that we had chosen wisely.

Now it may be the case that this sort of judgment is precisely the sort that the moral modesty advocated in chapter 8 would tell us we are in no position to make. This is clearly a legitimate question to raise; however, it is not quite so clear that moral modesty really does demand that we remain mute on such large evaluative judgments. All that moral modesty demands is that we recognize that there are likely evaluative facts that we do not grasp because our intellects are fallible and finite. Still, as strong as my intuition is that the natural environment is good on the whole, I must admit that it is a judgment of such scope that the strength of the intuition must at least be tempered by the realization that what we do not know about nature is far greater than what we do. So while I am not sure which wins in the end—the strength of the intuition that nature is of value or the modesty imposed on this judgment by its sweeping scope—the point of greatest moment for the present inquiry is the following: If the perspective of moral modesty wins the day and we refrain from the pretense of believing we can judge that nature is valuable on the whole, then we have good reason to be suspicious of the sorts of evaluative and modal judgments that must be made for the problem of evil to carry the day.

## Outweighing Evil

On October 31, 1999, an EgyptAir 767 crashed into the Atlantic and killed all 217 on board. Predictably, the media engaged in intense speculation concerning possible causes of the crash. Though the National Transportation Safety Board (NTSB) is yet to make an official declaration on the matter as of this writing, evidence retrieved from the cockpit voice recorder has been interpreted by some as evidence against believing that flight 990 went down as a result of a mechanical failure. The evidence is a prayer, "*Tawakilt ala Allah*" ("I put my trust in God"), that the copilot uttered shortly before the plane's autopilot was disengaged and it went into its catastrophic dive. It is also alleged that he repeated the prayer no less than fourteen times in the course of the plane's plunge. Given the timing of the initial utterance of the prayer and given that no evidence of any mechanical malfunction has been found, it has been widely suggested that the plane did not crash as a result of any mechanical problem. On this theory, the most likely explanation for the plane's going down is that it was the result of a deliberate act by the copilot. Now while the reports of the copilot's behavior, if true, are disturbing, there are at least two considerations that one would want to take into account before concluding that his behavior is conclusive evidence against the theory that some mechanical failure was the cause of the crash. At present it is unclear what the official verdict will be concerning the cause of the crash, but it is easy to see that there are two distinct ways that the evidence against a mechanical failure might be overridden. First, reasons might be brought to bear to show that the copilot's repeated prayer is not really evidence that the crash was a deliberate act. One reason might include the fact that "*Tawakilt ala Allah*" is a common prayer that would not be unusual for a Muslim to intersperse in his daily chores. Indeed, given that this is so, it might be very natural for one who was about to assume the controls of an airliner to put his trust in God. And the fact, if a fact it is, that he repeated the prayer as the plane plunged for the Atlantic, is hardly a surprising fact. That a man of faith gave voice to his faith in a time of crisis is hardly evidence of criminal intent. But perhaps what the cockpit voice recorder captured is as seriously incriminating as some have suggested. Perhaps the tone of utterance or a nuance of intonation renders the foregoing speculation about the naturalness of the prayer implausible. Perhaps, in the end, there will be no innocent explanation for the copilot's words; yet even if this is so, this does not mean that this evidence against the malfunction theory is decisive, for there is a second way it might be overridden. It may yet come to pass that a soon-to-be-retrieved piece of wreckage will be what NTSB investigators call a golden nugget that reveals clearly that there was a catastrophic malfunction in one of the plane's components. In such an event, we may be no clearer on why the copilot prayed when he did and as he did; nonetheless, it would be dubious at that point to still adhere to the view that the copilot's words show that the plane most likely did not crash as a result of a mechanical failure.[3]

The point that I want to draw out of this discussion of the evidentiary weight of the copilot's words is the following: Before one concludes that some specific evidence refutes a certain belief, one should do two things. First, one should evaluate the strength of the evidence. One should consider, that is, whether there are factors that reveal that the evidence is really not, after all, evidence against the belief in question or which reveal that the evidence is not as strong as it at first seemed. Second, one must consider whether there is independent evidence for the belief in question. This applies no less to the evidence against theism constituted by evil than it does to the evidence against a mechanical failure constituted by the copilot's words. That there are thus two considerations is significant at present because the preceding chapters of this book have been devoted exclusively to the first of these. All the explanations and stories told therein have been driving for one of two ends: (1) showing that it is reasonable to believe that God could have prevented some evil only by risking the loss of some greater good or (2) showing that we simply do not know what we would need to know in order to judge reliably that some evil is such that God could have prevented it without forfeiting some good of equal or greater value. What this means, however, is that I have completely neglected the second. And what *this* means is that even if the arguments offered in chapters 5 through 9 fail and there are none better to take their place, this still does not justify the conclusion that theism has lost intellectual respectability.[4] The simple reason that this is so is that there may well be independent evidence for theism that outweighs the evidence that unanswered evil poses to theism.

And that, of course, is the significance of the point made in the first section of this chapter. In working through the problem of evil, one must not overlook the fact that there is much good in the universe. This is so not simply for the reason that the good is arguably tied to the evil in important ways, but also because the goodness of the world is in no less a need of explanation than its evil. And if it is so clear that evil counts as evidence against the world's creation by God, then perhaps the goodness of the world counts as prima facie evidence for the world's creation by God.[5] Now this is a far cry from compelling evidence for God's existence; however, it does illustrate the fact that even if the problem of evil cannot be explained away, it might be counterbalanced or overwhelmed by independent evidence for theism. What this means is that this book has only begun the task of critically evaluating the problem of evil. A full treatment of the problem should also evaluate the weight of the various arguments for God's existence that philosophers and theologians continue to refine, defend, and criticize. It should also evaluate the weight of evidence other than evil against God's existence that might be brought to bear. In this book I proceeded as if the independent evidence for and against God's existence were equal. I did so not because I in fact believe that this is the case; rather, I did so because I believed it to be unnecessary to independently defend theism in order to reply to the problem of evil. If you decide that I was wrong and yet you are committed to theism or committed to giving theism a fair hearing, well, suffice it to say, you have a bit of work ahead of you.[6]

# Notes

## Introduction

1. This account of the Sanriku tsunami of 1896 is based on the report in Akitune Imamura's *Theoretical and Applied Seismology*, trans. D. Kennedy, 128–130.

2. For more on this practice see Philip Gourevitch's *We Wish to Inform You that Tomorrow We Will Be Killed with Our Families*, 202.

3. Sarah Ban Breathnach, *Simple Abundance: A Daybook of Comfort and Joy*, the entry for March 7.

4. See Part I, chapter 2 of George Orwell's *The Road to Wigan Pier*.

5. Manichaeism, certain offshoots of Zoroastrianism (such as the Zervanite sect), and some forms of Gnosticism all seem to fall into this category. For those interested in reading more about such religions, a good place to start is the *Encyclopedia of Religion*, ed. Mircea Eliade.

6. This is frequently referred to as the Orthodox Judaeo-Christian conception of God because of its prominence within this tradition. Despite its aptness in this respect, such labeling of the operative notion of God is misleading in two respects. First, it assumes greater unanimity of belief among Jewish and Christian denominations than in fact is the case. Second, it encourages overlooking the fact that roughly the same notion of God can be found in other religions, such as Islam and certain traditional African faiths. For this reason I will refrain from referring to this view of God as the Orthodox Judaeo-Christian view.

7. Thomas Aquinas (1225–1274), a Dominican philosopher and theologian, drew upon Aristotle's philosophy to explain and support the tenets of the Christian worldview. In addition to his monumental works on philosophy and theology, the *Summa Theologiae* and the *Summa Contra Gentiles*, Aquinas wrote numerous commentaries on Aristotle's philosophy.

8. This passage is from the *Summa Theologiae* (I, Q25, A.3) trans. Fathers of the English Dominican Province.

## Chapter One

1. This account of Sallee and Rumsey's flight from the Mann Gulch fire and Rumsey's words after the fact are taken from Norman Maclean's account of the tragedy in *Young Men and Fire*, 107.

2. Ibid., 106–123.

3. J.L. Mackie, "Evil and Omnipotence" in *Mind* 64 (1955): 200–212. This article is also reproduced in *The Problem of Evil*, ed. Marilyn McCord Adams and Robert Adams.

4. Some writers on the problem of evil make a distinction between bringing

about goods and preventing evils. With this distinction in place, one might revise the principle along the following lines: A good being will prevent any evil it can prevent unless it could not prevent the evil without forfeiting something at least as good or bringing about something at least as evil. For simplicity's sake, however, I will simply treat the prevention of evil as one kind of good that needs to be considered when one is evaluating what goods would be forfeited by preventing some evil. One example of a more carefully constructed set of conditions for the legitimate allowance of evil one could prevent is William Rowe's in "The Problem of Evil and Some Varieties of Atheism" in *The Problem of Evil*, ed. Adams and Adams, 126–137. There Rowe identifies the following three distinct conditions that might be alleged to justify an omninatured God (OG) in permitting some evil (s) that it could prevent: "(i) there is some greater good, G, such that G is obtainable by OG only if OG permits s1, or (ii) there is some greater good, G, such that G is obtainable by OG only if OG permits either s1 or some evil equally bad or worse, or (iii) s1 is such that it is preventable by OG only if OG permits some evil equally bad or worse." (128) One difference between my position and Rowe's is found in his insistence that condition (iii) is not included in condition (i). This amounts to rejecting my willingness to treat the prevention of evil as a kind of good. Now there may be good reason not to go the route I have gone; however, Rowe's not following this line is, it seems to me, based on a confusion. The reason that he gives for concluding that (iii) is not included in (i) is that "the absence of a good state of affairs need not itself be an evil state of affairs." (129) While this latter claim is certainly true, it does not show that (iii) is not included in (i). That the absence of a good state of affairs is not always evil merely shows that (i) is not included in (iii). What is needed to show that (iii) is not included in (i) is a case of an evil being prevented from befalling some being where this would not count as a good. It is, I believe, a mistake to try to build too much precision into one's principles at the outset. What qualifications are needed are best brought out in the give and take of argumentative discourse. An attempt to forestall such give and take at the outset often contributes only to obscurity and confusion.

5. This response to the logical version of the problem of evil has a long and illustrious history, dating back at least to Augustine in the fourth century A.D. We can find Augustine tracing evil to a will that is not caused to do evil by anything other than itself. In Book XII, chapter 6 of *The City of God*, for instance, he asks what the efficient cause of a bad will might be and concludes that it is nothing other than the will itself. But this does not mean, he writes in chapter 5 of *The Nature of the Good*, that creation would be better if it lacked free beings and thus evil free beings, for "corrupt gold is assuredly better than incorrupt silver, and corrupt silver than incorrupt lead; so also in more powerful spiritual natures a rational spirit even corrupted through an evil will is better than an irrational though incorrupt [spirit]." (*The Essential Augustine*, ed. Vernon J. Bourke, 50.) Notable advocates since Augustine include Saint Bonaventure, Saint Thomas Aquinas, and more recently, C.S. Lewis and Alvin Plantinga. It is Plantinga who is generally given credit for developing a satisfactory response to the logical problem of evil as formulated by J.L. Mackie. His formulation of the free will defense will constitute a large portion of chapter 3 of this work. For a nice survey

of advocates of the free will defense, see John Hick's *Evil and the God of Love*. It should be noted here that Hick's book is of interest for more than historical reasons. It is arguably the most formidable attempt to address the problem of evil in terms first proposed by Saint Irenaeus. It is also arguably one of the most substantial treatments of the problem of evil offered in twentieth-century philosophy. Hick's Irenaean approach will be considered in chapter 7 of this work.

6. While this definition is adequate for the purposes of this text, the task of arriving at a suitable technical definition of determinism is rather involved. For an excellent discussion of the difficulties involved in arriving at a precise definition, see chapter 1 of John Earman's *A Primer on Determinism*, 1986.

7. An accessible yet carefully reasoned defense of this claim can be found in Peter van Inwagen's *An Essay on Free Will*, 190–202.

8. This might seem like an understatement insofar as some would allege that quantum mechanics has shown that the behavior of subatomic particles is positively indeterministic. This, however, seems to me a stronger position than is actually warranted. For one thing, it is at least an open possibility that quantum indeterminacy is only an epistemic indeterminacy; that is, an indeterminacy only in *what we can know* about the subatomic world. It thus may not imply a metaphysical indeterminacy; that is, an indeterminacy in *the way things really are* in the subatomic world. An excellent discussion of determinism and the natural sciences is John Earman's *A Primer on Determinism*, mentioned earlier. To get a sense for the complexity of the issue of what quantum mechanics implies for determinism, see especially chapter 11. One of the interesting things about Earman's book is his contention that Newtonian science is not the bastion of determinism it is typically taken to be, whereas quantum mechanics is not as unequivocally anti-deterministic as it is often taken to be.

9. Instrumentalism is but one so-called antirealist account of the nature of scientific theories. Others are conventionalism and constructive empiricism. A good introduction to the realism/antirealism debate in the philosophy of science is chapter 4 of Arthur Zucker's *Introduction to the Philosophy of Science*. For a concise defense of the view that deterministic scientific theories do not rule out the possibility of free will, see Pierre Duhem's "The Physics of a Believer" (translated by Philip Wiener and appended to Wiener's translation of Duhem's *The Aim and Structure of Physical Theory*, 285–287). To conclude that there is no free will because the mathematical representations used in physical theories are deterministic, says Duhem, would be like "a collector who wishes to arrange sea shells. He takes seven drawers that he marks with seven colors of the spectrum, and you see him putting the red shells in the red drawer, the yellow shells in the yellow drawer, etc. But if a white shell appears, he will not know what to do with it, for he has no white drawer. You would, of course, feel very sorry for his reason if you heard him conclude in his embarrassment that no white shells exist in the world." (Duhem, 287)

10. "Libertarianism" as it is used here is a metaphysical theory about the nature of human actions. It is not to be confused with the political theory of the same name, which maintains that human liberty is a fundamental value that governments should be extremely loathe to restrict.

# Chapter Two

1. Despite what was said earlier about the indeterminist leanings of contemporary science, I will continue to speak of compatibilism as embracing determinism. Whether contemporary science makes this strong version of compatibilism unlikely is irrelevant to present concerns where the issue is whether this strong version of compatibilism is a logically coherent account of freedom. If it is, then it can be used to maintain that God could have caused human beings to always do what is right without actually violating their freedom. Whether or not determinism is actually true is irrelevant to this issue. Moreover, it is also worth noting here that even if quantum indeterminacy refutes determinism, other versions of compatibilism will still be viable options. Though I will continue to speak of compatibilism in terms of a thoroughgoing determinism, all a compatibilist theory really requires is that human actions be identified as free only to the extent that they are the product of certain kinds of causes; that is, the extent to which actions are undetermined plays no role in explaining their being done freely. Whether the aforementioned causes follow exceptionless or merely probable laws is in this sense irrelevant to the essence of the compatibilist's position. What the truth of indeterminism does do to the compatibilist's position is invalidate the antilibertarian argument that libertarianism cannot be true because determinism is true. But the failure of this one argument does not thereby automatically amount to a refutation of compatibilism and thus neither does the fact of indeterminism if a fact it is.

2. I do not want to give the reader the impression that my brothers teased me mercilessly. I can remember far more times when they were patient and solicitous playmates. In fact, I can remember one time in particular when one of my brothers—we'll call him Tom so as not to embarrass him—asked me if I wanted to play football with him and his friends. As I was only seven and not yet familiar with professional football rosters, he even told me the name of a player that I could pretend to be, a sort of playground nom de guerre as it were. So it was that whenever I got the ball, I would shout "Here comes Brazen Hussy!" Perhaps that wasn't the best example. But trust me, they were good brothers all.

3. So intimate is the connection between freedom and moral responsibility that many philosophers have seen fit to argue for freedom based on the fact that it is appropriate to hold human beings morally responsible for their actions. It was in this spirit that Aquinas wrote, "Man has free will: otherwise counsels, exhortations, commands, prohibitions, rewards and punishments would be in vain." (ST, I, 83, 1, resp.) The translation is taken from the *Summa Theologicae*.

4. I am here treating a decision to do nothing as an action. Let us suppose there is a father who, worried about spilling his beer, does not prevent his one-year-old from toddling down a flight of stairs. The father's inaction in this case satisfies the Ownership Condition insofar as he was the cause of the inaction as a conscious, reflective person. (This example also makes clear that I am using "reflective" as a descriptive and not an honorific term.) Also noteworthy is the fact that the Ownership Condition be formulated in terms of persons and not human beings. To see why, consider the case of a person who undergoes a sei-

zure at a restaurant and overturns a neighboring table in the course of thrashing about. There is a sense in which the human being undergoing the seizure is the causal source of the table's overturning; however, he is not the source of the action qua person. It is not something that he chose to do as a conscious, reflective being.

5. In the course of defending his own version of compatibilism, eighteenth-century British philosopher David Hume has put this point far more eloquently than I have.

> Actions are, by their very nature, temporary and perishing; and where they proceed not from some cause in the character and disposition of the person who performed them, they can neither redound to his honour, if good, nor infamy, if evil. The actions themselves may be blamable; they may be contrary to all the rules of morality and religion: But the person is not answerable for them; and as they proceeded from nothing in him that is durable and constant, and leave nothing of that nature behind them, it is impossible he can, upon their account, become the object of punishment or vengeance. According to the principle, therefore, which denies necessity, and consequently causes, a man is as pure and untainted, after having committed the most horrid crime, as at the first moment of his birth, nor is his character anywise concerned in his actions, since they are not derived from it, and the wickedness of the one can never be used as a proof of the depravity of the other (*Enquiry Concerning Human Understanding*, Section VIII, Part II).

6. Roderick Chisholm also has used the notion of avoidability in expressing roughly the same condition on moral responsibility. Whereas I have spoken of avoiding actions or states of affairs, Chisholm formulates what I am calling the Avoidability Condition as a principle about choice: "If a choice is one we could not have avoided making then it is one for which we are not morally responsible." Chisholm finds this principle so plausible that he suggests that it "may be interpreted as a logical truth." See his "Responsibility and Avoidability" in *Determinism and Freedom in the Age of Modern Science*, ed. Sidney Hook, 157.

7. I am here assuming that one's freely choosing to bring about an action or state of affairs is part of the action or state of affairs in question. The importance of this assumption is found in the following kind of case. I am standing on the South Summit, some 800 vertical feet below the summit of Mount Everest, attempting to become the only person to summit both Everest and K2 within a continuous two-week span. But I notice that famed high altitude climber Lynn "Matterhorn" Monty is a mere one hundred yards below me and gaining quickly. She also has just climbed K2 and is in danger of thwarting my achievement. Thus it is that I decide to cause an avalanche by stomping on a fragile snowbank poised above her. Though I did not know it, the lip was going to fall prey to the force of gravity in the next moment anyway, and thus I was in no position to prevent Matterhorn Monty from being swept away by the avalanche. Nonetheless, my action still does satisfy the Avoidability Condition in that I had it within

my power to prevent the action that consisted in *my* deliberately causing the avalanche.

Some readers may here suspect that this assumption is partly an attempt to sidestep the issues raised in Harry Frankfurt's now classic attack on what he calls the principle of alternate possibilities. Such readers would be right in their suspicions. The principle of alternate possibilities maintains that "a person is morally responsible for what he has done only if he could have done otherwise." (Harry Frankfurt, "Alternate Possibilities and Moral Responsibility" in *The Journal of Philosophy,* 829–839.) This principle, which obviously resembles what I have called the Avoidability Condition, is rejected by Frankfurt because it does not handle cases in which an individual (Black) chooses to perform some action even though a second person (Jones) is ready to do what is needed—via hypnosis, perhaps—to make Black choose the action should he show signs of wavering. I will not spend significant time discussing Frankfurt's attack on the principle of alternate possibilities. Though it is an ingenious piece of philosophizing, it seems to me that it is an example of what might be called a "specious rigor." What I am calling specious rigor occurs when we have a principle that we find intuitively very plausible, and we are encouraged to abandon it on the basis of counterexamples that involve either *(a)* counterintuitive assumptions, *(b)* assumptions about which our intuitions are mute, ambivalent, or uncertain or (c) a failure to define key terms that are crucial to deciding whether to accept the counterexample. In the case of Frankfurt's counterexamples, for instance, an unstated and hence unargued for assumption is that a choice that is a product of an individual's unfettered deliberation is the same kind of event as a choice that is produced by hypnosis or chemical manipulation. Only if we make this assumption does Frankfurt's counterexample refute the version of the principle that I have proposed, a version in which the free choice that causes an act should be viewed as part of the act or state of affairs to be avoided. It seems to me, moreover, that there is no good reason to buy into the needed assumption. Frankfurt might respond, of course, that we do not need to buy into the assumption that I find dubious provided we are willing to believe that the choice that prompts an action is not part of the "doing" with which the principle of alternate possibilities is concerned. But why should we accept this assumption? It seems to me a strange assumption to make in a principle that is intended to be about moral responsibility. Indeed, Frankfurt gives us no reason to accept this assumption insofar as he does not "consider in what sense the concept of 'could have done otherwise' figures in the principle of alternate possibilities." (Frankfurt, 834) Moreover, this assumption would mean that Frankfurt's counterexample does not touch a version of the avoidability condition, like Chisholm's, which formulates the principle in terms of the avoidability of choice. But perhaps Frankfurt wants us to believe that this is irrelevant to the counterexample because Black is never given the chance to decide not to do the action. Jones knows what Black will decide in advance of Black's making the decision. This means that if Jones were to intervene, it could be done before Black had the chance to decide against performing the action. And this means that even if we suppose the manipulated action to be different from the freely chosen action, it does not count as Black's "doing" otherwise, for it is not by any "doing" of Black's that the "otherwise" has come about. This is roughly how Martha Klein defends Frankfurt's counterexamples from an objection much like the one I have been raising. (Martha Klein, *Determinism, Blameworthiness and Deprivation,* 32–33.) But the problem then becomes that it is hard to give content to Jones's ability to predict what Black will choose unless one assumes that the agent's choices are causally determined. And why should a libertarian assume that? On the other hand, if we back off the certainty with which Jones can predict and say that Black's showing a nondeterministic inclination to decide not to do the action is what prompts Jones' intervention, we must still wonder whether Black's culpability might not be found in the fact that he did not even take the first step that would be involved in his deciding otherwise. Now, I'm not at all clear as to what I want to say about such issues. What is clear to me, however, is that it would be silly to let such implausible and conceptually unrefined examples lead me to give up a principle that is intuitively highly plausible and applies in any case that might realistically be encountered.

8. An excellent defense of libertarian freedom that contains an extended development and defense of this argument can be found in chapter 3 of Peter van Inwagen's *An Essay on Free Will.*

9. Walter Stace defends this version of the principle in *Religion and the Modern Mind.* See especially pp. 248–258. (The relevant material from Stace can also be found in *An Introduction to Modern Philosophy: Examining the Human Condition*, A. Castell, D. Borchert, and A. Zucker, 110–118.)

10. I have developed the compatibilist's reply here on the assumption that she would dig in her heels on the demand for avoidability at the level of choice. There is no reason, however, that she might not do so further down the line—at the level of desire or deliberation, perhaps. What is clear, however, is that at some point she will have to dig in her heels, and at that point will most likely fall back on the notion of act ownership to make sense of moral responsibility.

11. The point I am making here is very similar to that made by Paul Edwards in "Hard and Soft Determinism" in Sidney Hook *Determinism and Freedom in the Age of Modern Science,* 117–125. Edwards writes that "the reflective person . . . requires not only that the agent was not coerced; he also requires that the agent originally chose his own character—the character that now displays itself in his choices and desires and efforts." (123)

12. C.J. Ducasse takes this route in his essay "Determinism, Freedom, and Responsibility." "That a person P is now morally responsible for his voluntary acts," he writes, "means simply that to praise or blame him or otherwise reward or punish him for some thing he now does or did will tend to cause him to act, or tend to inhibit him from acting, in a similar manner on similar future occasions." (Sidney Hook 1974, 168).

13. Though his account is more nuanced than I here have space to delve into, it is worth noting that John Stuart Mill embraces roughly this view where he writes that "the sentiment of justice appears to me to be, the animal desire to repel or retaliate a hurt or damage to oneself, or to those with whom one sympathizes, widened so as to include all persons, by the human capacity of enlarged

sympathy, and the human conception of intelligent self-interest. From the latter elements, the feeling derives its morality; from the former, its peculiar impressiveness, and energy of self-assertion" (John Stuart Mill, *Utilitarianism*, in *Utilitarianism, On Liberty and Essay on Bentham*, ed. Mary Warnock, 308).

## Chapter Three

1. This is even true of some philosophers who defend libertarian freedom. Consider the following remarks by Peter van Inwagen: "I find the concept of immanent or agent causation puzzling, as I suspect most of my readers do (those who don't find it downright incoherent). In fact, I find it more puzzling than the problem it is supposed to be a solution to. Obscurum per obscurius!" (Peter van Inwagen, *An Essay on Free Will*, 151).

2. This point, I take it, is the gist of the following remarks made by the seventeenth-century French philosopher René Descartes to Pierre Gassendi, a materialist who questioned Descartes's assertion that the will is free. The various claims that he made about the will's freedom are, Descartes said, "the sorts of things that each of us ought to know by experience in his own case, rather than having to be convinced of them by rational argument; and you, O Flesh, do not seem to attend to the actions the mind performs within itself. You may be unfree, if you wish; but I am certainly very pleased with my freedom since I experience it within myself" (CSM, II, 259; AT, VII, 377).

3. A.J. Ayer puts the matter thus: "Either it is an accident that I choose to act as I do or it is not. If it is an accident, then it is merely a matter of chance that I did not choose otherwise; and if it is merely a matter of chance that I did not choose otherwise, it is surely irrational to hold me morally responsible for choosing as I did. But if it is not an accident that I choose to do one thing rather than another, then presumably there is some causal explanation of my choice: and in that case we are led back to determinism." (A.J. Ayer, *Philosophical Essays*, 275).

4. To get a sense for the kind of complexities involved, a good place to start would be chapter 8 of John Earman's *A Primer on Determinism*.

5. Van Inwagen approaches the matter this way on pp. 128–129 of his *An Essay on Free Will*. Though I have no quarrel with what van Inwagen says there, it does seem to me that to approach the Chance Objection as he does is to miss the real source of its force.

6. These examples may well remind some readers of recent philosophical discussion of moral luck. A nice piece on moral luck that can serve as an introduction to the topic is Andrew Latus's "Moral and Epistemic Luck " in the *Journal of Philosophical Research*.

7. A very different approach to solving the chance objection is Robert Kane's "Responsibility, Luck, and Chance: Reflections on Free Will and Indeterminism" in *The Journal of Philosophy*, 217–240. Whereas I have been interested in showing that the notion of chance that is exculpating is simply not present in a libertarian free choice, Kane devotes his effort to showing that moral responsi-

bility can tolerate a certain measure of chance or indeterminacy between the agent's intention and the outcome for which he is responsible.

## Chapter Four

1. J.L. Mackie may have this objection in mind when he writes that "if there is no logical impossibility in a man's freely choosing the good on one, or on several, occasions, there cannot be a logical impossibility in his freely choosing the good on every occasion. God was not, then, faced with a choice between making innocent automata and making beings who, in acting freely, would sometimes go wrong; there was open to him the obviously better possibility of making beings who would act freely but always go right." (J.L. Mackie, "Evil and Omnipotence," in *The Problem of Evil*, ed. Adams and Adams, 33.) I say that Mackie "may have" this objection in mind because as he develops this point, he does not distinguish it from what I have called the challenge of compatibilism and the chance objection against libertarianism. Insofar as the atheist's objection that I am currently developing concedes libertarian freedom, it is distinct both from the challenge of compatibilism and the chance objection.

2. I here ignore the possibility that God might have given human beings the ability to choose between good and evil but then stood ever ready to see to it that all human decisions to do evil are thwarted. I decide to have an affair, but I find myself—despite my will—acting so as to be faithful to my wife. There are, it seems to me, two things that a theist might say about this type of objection. The first is that the choice to do evil, though ultimately impotent, is an evil in itself; regardless of whether evil consequences flow from it or not. Certainly the man who resolves to commit evil is guilty of evil intent even if the opportunity to act on the intent never arises. Imagine a man who is stranded on an island, doomed to live out the rest of his life there. He also happens to be a man who has long nurtured feelings of jealousy against one of his brothers, a brother who has been guilty of nothing other than well-earned success. Just before the jealous brother became marooned, he resolved that he would engineer the successful brother's downfall, spreading vicious rumors about him and falsely implicating him in illegal financial dealings. Now the marooned brother will never have the opportunity to act on this evil intent; nonetheless, the evil intent in its own right is a privation of the love that ought to hold between brothers and is something that ought not to be. It ought not to be because it is evil. It may well be that an evil intent that is realized is part of an action that is much more evil than one that is unrealized; nonetheless, this does not call into question the fact that the unrealized evil intent is evil in its own right. Second, it is not clear that the psychology involved in such a scenario ultimately makes sense. Though I do not have the space to develop the point here, the basic problem is that such beings would very quickly learn that none of their evil intentions were realized and this realization would soon lead them to stop forming evil intentions—a de facto diminution of their freedom. If, on the other hand, they did continue to formulate evil intentions, we might then wonder whether intentions formed with the knowledge that they will not be realized are intentions at all.

3. Readers familiar with Alvin Plantinga's writings on the problem of evil will recognize this as Plantinga's concept of "weak actualization." For more on this concept, see his "God, Evil, and the Metaphysics of Freedom" in *The Problem of Evil,* ed. Adams and Adams, 83–109.

4. A nice introduction to and argument for the incoherence of middle knowledge is Robert Adams's "Middle Knowledge and the Problem of Evil" in *The Problem of Evil*, Adams and Adams, 110–125. Much of my own discussion of middle knowledge is indebted to Robert Adams's work on the topic.

## Chapter Five

1. An example of a logical connection between the antecedent and the consequent would be "If $x$ is a prime number greater than ten, then $x$ is an odd number." An example of a conditional expressing a causal connection would be "if this sugar cube is submerged in a nonsaturated solution of water, then it will dissolve."

2. Given the problems attendant to offering a coherent account of middle knowledge, one might well wonder what has led some philosophers to embrace it. In my estimation it is partly motivated by a confusion that tends to skew our intuitions in favor of its possibility. The confusion I have in mind is evident in Alvin Plantinga's handling of the following counterfactuals of freedom: *(a)* If Curley had been offered $20,000, he would have accepted the bribe; and *(b)* If Curley had been offered $20,000, he would have rejected the bribe. (In Plantinga's imaginary scenario, Curley has accepted a bribe of $35,000 and his acceptance led others to wonder if Curely might have sold out more cheaply.) Whether one of these counterfactuals is true, says Plantinga, really amounts to the question of "whether there is something Curley would have done had this state of affairs been actual." And the answer to this question is, for Plantinga, "obvious and affirmative" for it is simply clear as can be that "there is something that Curley would have done, had that state of affairs obtained." (Alvin Plantinga, "God, Evil, and the Metaphysics of Freedom" in *The Problem of Evil*, ed. Adams and Adams, 97.) But Plantinga's contention here ignores the fact that the counterfactual the truth of which he takes to be obvious is the following: "If Curley had been offered $20,000, either he would have rejected the bribe or he would have accepted the bribe." I agree that this counterfactual is obviously true, if only for the reason that its consequent is a tautology and hence necessarily true; however, it seems to me that it is illicit to move from the truth of this counterfactual to the requirement that one of the following be true: *(a)* If Curley had been offered $20,000, then he would have accepted the bribe; or *(b)* If Curley had been offered $20,000, then he would have rejected the bribe. That Curley would either do or not do a certain action under certain circumstances is clear enough; however, it is not at all clear that there is a connection either between the circumstances and Curley's doing the action or between the circumstances and Curley's not doing the action. There may only be a connection between the circumstances and his doing one of the two alternatives without it being specified *which* of the alternatives he would do. Here is an imperfect analogy to explain what I have in mind.

Imagine that a coin toss is a metaphysically indeterminate event. In that case, we would be happy to say that "if the coin had been tossed, it would either come up heads or not heads" without thereby committing ourselves to the truth of one of the following conditionals: *(a)* if the coin had been tossed, it would have been heads; or *(b)* if the coin had been tossed, it would not have been heads. Thus it is that there would be a connection between the coin's being tossed and (an indeterminate) one of the two outcomes obtaining without there being a connection between the coin's having been tossed and specifically which of the two outcomes would prevail. That one of them would have obtained is fixed, but which one of them would have obtained is not fixed. It should be noted that moving from the counterfactual with the disjunctive consequent to the disjunct of the two counterfactuals is legitimate if we treat the counterfactuals as straightforward material conditionals; however, the problems with attempting to treat counterfactuals—let alone counterfactuals of freedom—as material conditions are too significant to countenance relying on a material conditional analysis in making the move from one to the other. Here, I submit, we can do no better than rely on our more immediate intuitions on the logical implications of the relevant counterfactuals.

3. Plantinga has more recently formulated a version of this argument that does not depend upon the assumption that God has middle knowledge, but only upon the assumption that subjunctives of freedom have a truth value. In response to the objection that God's not knowing such propositions would compromise God's omniscience, Plantinga writes the following: "One who holds that there are counterfactuals of freedom but no middle knowledge on the part of God will hold, presumably, that middle knowledge is not possible; he will then reconstrue omniscience as knowledge, not of the truth values of all propositions there are, but of all propositions such that knowledge of their truth values is possible." (Alvin Plantinga, "Self-Profile" in *Alvin Plantinga*, ed. James Tomberlin and Peter van Inwagen, 96). But notice what happens if one goes this route; namely, the need for Plantinga's deployment of the notion of transworld depravity evaporates. For on this understanding of middle knowledge and omniscience, it is open to the theist to say the following: Since God does not know which counterfactuals of freedom are true and which false, God cannot be reasonably expected to know how to create a world in which all free creatures always refrain from doing evil. But if this is so, then it may well be that *(a)* there are possible worlds that contain moral good but no moral evil, and *(b)* it was within God's power to weakly actualize one of these worlds by strongly actualizing the antecedent of the relevant subjunctive conditional; but that God cannot be blamed for not actualizing one of these worlds for the simple reason that it is not possible to know the relevant counterfactual of freedom. Thus it is that Plantinga's going the route of transworld depravity really is a kind of casting of his lot with middle knowledge. Moreover, it seems to me that this is the route any philosopher should go who is willing to grant that subjunctive conditionals of freedom have truth values. For any theist who holds that there are propositions that have truth values and that God cannot know these truth values owes us some account of what it is about the propositions in question that makes it reasonable to suppose that such propositions are

unknowable in a sense that does not compromise God's omniscience. There may well be some such account, but I cannot think of what it might be. The most likely strategy would be to devise some argument about the act of knowing that mirrors the argument constructed in chapter four about the act of doing. But the problem is that the *knowing* of some state of affairs is not a fact about the state of affairs in the way in which the *doing* of some state of affairs is a fact about the state of affairs.

4. Though I will not pursue this line of defense in this work, it is, I believe, a more respectable position than is typically conceded. Its proponents include philosophers of no less talent than Saint Augustine and Alvin Plantinga.

5. Though it is true that the balance of attention has shifted from logical to evidential versions of the problem of evil in the last twenty years, it needs to be noted that casting the problem of evil in probabilistic terms is not at all new. One of the most powerful formulations of this version of the problem of evil is that found in eighteenth-century British philosopher David Hume's *Dialogues Concerning Natural Religion*.

## Chapter Six

1. I realize that I'm being a bit unfair here, for I'm sure that the pros-and-cons approach is often suggested merely as a way of clarifying the factors that are bearing upon the decision. It may, indeed, have some benefit in this respect; though I must say that this is never the way it was presented to me. My reaction after going through the procedure was always to think: "Okay. Now what?"

2. Bayes's theorem: $P(A/B\&C) = P(A/C) \times P(B/A\&C)/P(B/C)$

A is the hypothesis in question and B is the evidence in question. C is the set of all other claims that are relevant and believed to be true—the background information. When this is applied to evil and theism, theism is substituted for A and some claim about the existence of evil is substituted for B. Applying Bayes's theorem to the problem of evil, then, would amount to making an estimation of the overall likelihood of theism in light of some fact about evil. For a nice accessible account of Bayes's theorem and its use in evidential versions of the problem of evil, see Robert Adams's "The Problem of Evil" in *Alvin Plantinga*, ed. James Tomberlin and Peter van Inwagen, 237–253.

3. Grahame's Mole from *The Wind in the Willows* is a most articulate proponent of the value of one's home. After a long absence, he catches the smell of his home and "with a rush of old memories, how clearly it stood up before him, in the darkness! Shabby indeed, and small and poorly furnished, and yet his, the home he had made for himself, the home he had been so happy to get back to after his day's work. And the home had been happy with him, too, evidently, and was missing him, and wanted him back, and was telling him so . . . ." Kenneth Grahame, *The Wind in the Willows*, 86.

4. Plato, "*Crito*," 48c-e, trans. G.M.A. Grube in *Five Dialogues*.

5. Immanuel Kant, *Grounding for the Metaphysics of Morals*, trans. James W. Ellington.

6. Advocates of the problem of evil, it seems to me, are sometimes guilty of wanting to have it both ways. When they speak of how easy it would be for God to create a world that is better than ours, they give omnipotence an almost completely unfettered leeway. But when a theist makes rather extravagant use of God's omnipotence in his theodicy, it is occasionally dismissed as wildly implausible.

7. French for "the arrow," the pharmacologist/inventor's pretentious reference to Cupid.

8. One might try to resist this conclusion by contending that the reason the drug-induced love is less prized is that it does not redound to one's genuine desirability in the way that spontaneous love does. If a man professes his love for his wife freely, one might reason, then the wife knows that it is traits about her that have won his affection. But if it is merely the drug that makes him want her, need her, desire her, then it is the drug and not something about her that makes him want, need, and desire her. But this, it seems to me, is a confusion, for even in the drug-induced version, it is traits about the woman that immediately cause the man to want, need, and desire her. Indeed, he can sincerely say that he finds the woman's smile irresistible, her taciturn manner dark and mysterious, and her willingness to have used the drug as a sign of her devotion to pursuing what she wants.

9. As opposed, say, to reasons of greed or fear or revenge.

10. Some apologists for theism would disagree with my position here and concede that the possibility of friendships and other love relationships between human beings would not necessarily be compromised by determinism. Nonetheless, they go on to defend the view that real freedom is a good by maintaining that if God were the author of a determinism that ruled human beings as well as the rest of the universe, then it would not be possible for God to enter into genuine love relationships with human beings. That would be, according to these philosophers, like a hypnotist having a true love relationship with a subject that he has hypnotically induced to have feelings of affection for him. Robert Adams, for one, has reasoned as follows:

> [O]ne of God's main purposes in creating the world was to have creatures who would be related to Him as His children and friends. The bearing of determinism on this purpose is not the same as its bearing on the significance of relationships among human beings. Even if determinism were known to be true it would not follow that your kindness to me or your injuring me are simply results of my manipulation. Therefore it might still be reasonable for me to thank you or blame you. That is one of the principal grounds for the compatibilist contention that the truth of determinism would not destroy our moral responsibility to each other. But God being the Creator of all other causal agents and the Author of all causal laws, everything that happens will be something that He has done, directly or indirectly, if determinism is true. The truth of determinism would undermine our moral responsibility to God, and He could not have a fully per-

sonal relationship with us. (Robert Adams, "The Problem of Evil" in *Alvin Plantinga*, ed. James E. Tomberlin and Peter Van Inwagen, 228).

Adams is here inspired by John Hick, who deploys roughly the same line of reasoning on p. 310 of his *Evil and a God of Love*. As should be evident at various points in this book, I have profited enormously from reading both Adams and Hick on the problem of evil; however, in this case I do not see the force of their argument. While there is certainly a distinction to be made between another's love for oneself that one has causally determined to be so and another's love for oneself that some third party has causally determined to be so, I see no reason for thinking that this distinction is relevant to the issue of whether the causally determined relationship would be real or artificial. If a hypnotist friend has hypnotically induced my wife to fall in love with me, I do not see how that makes her love for me any truer than if I had been the one who had cast the spell. The source of the causal determination of the affection seems to me utterly irrelevant to the value one might assign to the relationship. Adams's point might be taken to be an epistemic one; that is, if one does not do the manipulating oneself, then one might not know that the person's love was simply engineered. And if the person were ignorant of the manipulation, then he or she might value the others affection as much as if it were genuine. This seems to me a legitimate point, but it has nothing to do with who is the source of the manipulation, for the hypnotist could bring about the same effect by causing the woman to fall in love with him and then using his hypnotism to induce ignorance in himself of the fact that the woman's love had been causally induced. Moreover, Adams himself forecloses on such an epistemic reading when he says that "even if determinism were known to be true it would not follow that your kindness to me or your injuring me are simply results of *my* manipulation." And even if the epistemic interpretation is what Adams had in mind, it soon runs into difficulties itself. For one thing, it seems to me that one might argue that it is better to have genuine love than it is to have pseudo love even if one does not realize that one has the false variety. For another, one would then have to factor in the evil that is one's holding the false belief that the love is real.

## Chapter Seven

1. Some might think that talking of the "gears" of nature is an inapt metaphor given the tendency of contemporary physics to view nature as an indeterministic system. This, however, seems to me a mistake. First, if a realist interpretation of quantum indeterminacy is true, then it applies at the macro as well as the subatomic level. That is to say, machines would be subject to indeterminacy—albeit a vanishingly low indeterminacy—no less than electrons. I hardly think, however, that this fact would lead us to stop speaking of "gears" as being causally relevant at the macro level. Moreover, the analogy between mechanisms and the natural order does not only emphasize the regularity of nature. It also emphasizes the fact that both machines and nature seem to operate in the absence of any awareness of what they are doing.

2. One theodicy that develops this account of the value of a natural order can be found in Bruce Reichenbach's *Evil and a Good God*. An eminently readable version of this account can also be found in chapter 2 of C.S. Lewis's *The Problem of Pain*.

3. That this is why we take waking experience to be more real than dreamed experience has been advocated by numerous philosophers. In the Sixth Meditation of his *Meditations on First Philosophy*, for example, Descartes writes that there is a vast difference between waking experience and dreamed experience, a difference found in the fact "that dreams are never linked by memory with all the other actions of life as waking experiences are. If, while I am awake, anyone were suddenly to appear to me and then disappear immediately, as happens in sleep, so that I could not see where he had come from or where he had gone to, it would not be unreasonable for me to judge that he was a ghost, or a vision created in my brain, rather than a real man." (CSM, II, 61–62; AT, VII, 89–90) It is, for Descartes, the disorderliness of the experience that licenses the conclusion that dreams are less real. And if he is right about this, then all that is would be diminished to that lower level of reality if all were thus disorderly.

4. Second, even if we set aside concerns about the degree of reality of a disorderly environment, there is reason to wonder whether it makes sense to suppose that *we* might inhabit such an illusory realm. Some philosophers have maintained that we can only be aware of ourselves indirectly, by first being aware of an objective order of which we have direct experience. Perhaps the most notable advocate of this view is Immanuel Kant who argued in the *Critique of Pure Reason* that one can be conscious of oneself and one's subjective states only by knowing an objective order that is distinct from those states and from one's self. Now it would be folly to here undertake the daunting task of explaining let alone defending Kant's dense argument on this matter; nonetheless, it is worth noting that no less a philosopher than Immanuel Kant linked the possibility of self-consciousness with the experience of an objectively ordered environment. Readers interested in pursuing this point further should consult the Transcendental Deduction of Kant's *Critique of Pure Reason*.

5. I should here specify that I am referring to the Disney adaptation of C. Collodi's tale. There the Irenaean overtones are fairly explicit:

> And when the wand touched him Pinocchio came to life! First he blinked his eyes, then he raised his wooden arm and wiggled his jointed fingers. "I can move!" he cried. "I can talk!" "Yes, Pinocchio," the blue fairy smiled. "Geppetto needs a little son. So tonight I give you life." "Then I'm a real boy!" cried Pinocchio joyfully. "No," said the Fairy sadly. "There is no magic that can make us real. I have given you life—the rest is up to you." "Tell me what I must do," begged Pinocchio. "I want to be a real boy!" "Prove yourself brave, truthful, and unselfish," said the Blue Fairy. (*Pinocchio*, adapted by Dick Kelsey in *Walt Disney's Treasury*, 70.

6. This is not to say that one might not have a character conferred upon one that is similar to the character forged by one's free choices. It is to say, however,

that one's character in the former case would not be morally significant and thus would not be an appropriate object of respect or disdain, love or hate.

7. Augustine, *The Confessions*, Book I, Chapter 1.
8. C.S. Lewis, puts the matter thus:
   We can rest contentedly in our sins and in our stupidities; and anyone who has watched gluttons shoveling down the most exquisite foods as if they did not know what they were eating, will admit that we can ignore even pleasure. But pain insists upon being attended to. God whispers to us in our pleasures, speaks in our conscience, but shouts in our pains: it is His megaphone to rouse a deaf world. A bad man, happy, is a man without the least inkling that his actions do not "answer," that they are not in accord with the laws of the universe.

   —*The Problem of Pain*, 93.

9. John Beversluis, *C.S. Lewis and the Search for Rational Religion*, 117.
10. Lewis, *The Problem of Pain*, 68.
11. Lewis, 110.

## Chapter Eight

1. Norman Maclean, *Young Men and Fire*, 92–101.
2. In the last two to three decades, this approach to responding to evidential versions of the problem of evil has enjoyed quite a bit of popularity. Some of the recent essays that advocate some version of this approach can be found in Daniel Howard-Snyder's *The Evidential Argument from Evil*. See especially the articles by Alvin Plantinga, William Alston, Peter Van Inwagen, and Stephen Wykstra. To get a sense of the critical response that this approach has encountered, see the articles by William Rowe, Paul Draper, and Richard Gale, also in the Howard-Snyder volume.

The basic sentiment behind this response is not at all new. One can see it in Descartes's *Meditations on First Philosophy* where, in the course of recognizing that he cannot explain why God did not make him utterly immune from error, he writes that "it is no cause for surprise if I do not understand the reasons for some of God's actions; and there is no call to doubt his existence if I happen to find that there are other instances where I do not grasp why or how certain things were made by him." (CSM, II, 38; AT, VII, 55) Another place one can find this sentiment expressed is, of course, in the Book of Job.

3. I am sure that some readers will here wonder whether I am being consistent. I did, after all, defend in chapter 6 the conclusion that it is possible and appropriate to love God despite God's metaphysical invulnerability. It must be remembered, however, that the argument there turned on God's being vulnerable to our vulnerabilities. As the possibility of this indirect sort of vulnerability depends upon the presence of higher level cognition, this account cannot be applied to the case of babies and thus the question of their lovableness were they invulnerable remains. We could, of course, stipulate that the babies are born

brilliant, but then we'd have to wonder whether babies endowed with such cognitive powers from birth would really be human babies.

## Chapter Nine

1. Fyodor Dostoyevsky, *The Brothers Karamazov*, trans. Constance Garnett, 291.

2. Marilyn McCord Adams, "Horrendous Evils and the Goodness of God" in *The Problem of Evil*, ed. Adams and Adams, 217.

3. Ibid., 210.

4. Dostoyevsky, *The Brothers Karamazov*, 292.

5. Unlike Adams, who aligns herself with Ivan, were I to pick a character from literature who espouses a view close to mine on this matter, I might settle on Melville's Father Mapple, who concludes his sermon by proclaiming "I leave eternity to Thee; for what is man that he should live out the lifetime of his God?" (Herman Melville, *Moby Dick,* 51). This is not to say that I reject personal immortality. Nor is it to say that I believe there are no decisive philosophical reasons for believing in a personal afterlife. It is to say, however, that even if personal immortality were not in the cards for human beings, we would have no grounds to impugn God's goodness. And I would be willing to make the point more general and say that even if finite goods are all the goods human beings can expect, then there is still no reason to conclude that God is not good in a fairly normal sense of good. Nor is there reason not to view the created order, on balance, as a good thing.

6. One might, for instance believe that the good of being cured of cancer balances off the pain and suffering of chemotherapy. Nonetheless, the situation would be better still if there were an equally effective treatment that did not involve the suffering connected with chemotherapy. Thus it is that the suffering involved in the treatment is balanced off but not defeated by the cure. A case of an evil being defeated, on the other hand, would be the following: Sorrow is an evil; however, the presence of sorrow over another's undeserved misfortune actually makes the situation somewhat better than it would be if one felt no sorrow at the other's misfortune. (See Roderick Chisholm's "The Defeat of Good and Evil," in *The Problem of Evil,* eds. Adams and Adams, 53–68.)

7. For an explanation of this distinction, see Alvin Plantinga's "Self-Profile" in *Alvin Plantinga*, ed. James Tomberlin and Peter van Inwagen, 42.

8. Marilyn McCord Adams, "Horrendous Evils and the Goodness of God," in *The Problem of Evil,* 211. One might take Adams's "prima facie reason to doubt" as redundant in that a reason to doubt would already be earmarked as a reason that was prima facie and not decisive. If it were decisive, one might reason, then it would be a sufficient condition for believing that the sufferer's life is not good on the whole, as opposed to being a mere reason to doubt. This, however, is not necessarily the case. One way to see that there may be no redundancy is to note that the redundancy charge is equivalent to the claim that the phrase "absolute reason to doubt" is contradictory, a claim that does not seem to be well grounded. An absolute reason to doubt might, without undue idiosyncrasy, be

taken as a reason that provides evidence against some hypothesis, regardless of whatever other evidence is accumulated, where the evidence in question is not decisive. Even though an absolute reason to doubt could be outweighed by other evidence, it would never lose its evidentiary significance of counting against a certain belief. A prima facie reason to doubt, on the other hand, would be a reason that could be outweighed by other evidence but could also be muted by other evidence or even "flipped" in the context of other evidence so that what was a reason to doubt now becomes a reason to believe. Though she does not explain her use of "prima facie reason to doubt," I assume that Adams uses it in the sense just explained. For one thing, this fits her contention that uniquely Christian valuables make it possible for horrendous evils to be "defeated" in the Chisholmian sense within the context of an individual's life. Such "defeat" of horrendous evil, of course, would not have to be paired with the epistemic theory just discussed; however, it would be strange not to so pair it if only for the fact that in the enlightenment of the afterlife it would be very strange for defeated horrendous evil not to be seen as positive evidence for the goodness of one's life as a whole. "Defeated" evils in the afterlife would be seen as episodes that were actually working toward one's ultimate fulfillment. As such, an enlightened view of them would take them to actually be evidence for the goodness of one's life as a whole.

9. Indeed, she believes that any attempt to do so actually gives one less reason to believe in God's love and goodness with respect to individual human beings whose lives have been ravaged by horrendous evil (Adams, 214–215).

10. Marilyn McCord Adams, "Horrendous Evils and the Goodness of God" in *The Problem of Evil,* 214. A similar claim is made by William Alston in "The Inductive Argument from Evil," in *The Evidential Argument from Evil,* ed. Daniel Howard-Snyder, 111.

## Chapter Ten

1. A very nice discussion of the history of the ichneumonid's role in relation to considerations of nature's value can be found in Stephen Jay Gould's *Rocks of Ages,* 173–190.

2. This estimate of the number of species of plants and animals being lost annually is taken from Niles Eldredge's *Life in the Balance: Humanity and the Biodiversity Crisis,* vii.

3. The source for my account of the speculation—and I do want to stress that it is speculation—surrounding EgyptAir flight 990 is "The Inside Story of Flight 990" by Daniel Klaidman and Mark Hosenball in the November 29, 1999, issue of *Newsweek.*

4. I have, incidentally, confined my remark to those chapters confronting evidential versions of the problem for the reason that the second consideration that one must bring to bear against the evidence of evil would be idle were the logical version of the problem unanswerable. Fortunately for theists it is now conceded by almost all interested philosophers that the logical version of the problem is no longer a viable challenge to theism.

5. One, but not the only, way that this point has been made is by stressing

that the goodness or perfection of the universe admits of degrees of perfection that are intelligible only if there is some absolute standard that finite goods resemble to varying degrees. This, in fact, is the fourth of Aquinas's five ways. He puts the matter as follows:

> The fourth way is taken from the gradation to be found in things. Among beings there are some more and some less good, true, noble, and the like. But "more" and "less" are predicated of different things, according [as they resemble in their different ways something which is the maximum] as a thing is said to be hotter according as it more nearly resembles that which is hottest; so that there is something which is truest, something best, something noblest, and, consequently, something which is uttermost being; for those things are greatest in truth are greatest in being. . . . Now the maximum in any genus is the cause of all in that genus; as fire, which is the maximum of heat, is the cause of all hot things. Therefore there must also be something which is to all beings the cause of their being, goodness, and every other perfection; and this we call God" (*Summa Theologiae*, I, 1, 3).

6. A fine place to begin this work would be with Curtis Hancock and Brendan Sweetman's *Truth and Religious Belief: Conversations on Philosophy of Religion*. Another good place to start would be with question two of the first part of Aquinas's *Summa Theologiae*. There one will find Aquinas's five attempts to demonstrate God's existence (his "five ways") as well as his reasons for rejecting various other attempts to prove God's existence, the most notable of these being Saint Anselm's ontological argument. Though Aquinas was unconvinced by Anselm's argument, the ontological argument has been undergoing a revival of late, with contemporary innovations in modal logic being used to formulate putatively stronger versions of the argument. A good place to start considering contemporary versions of the ontological argument would be in Alvin Plantinga's *The Nature of Necessity*. A nice anthology that would serve as a general introduction to contemporary attempts to prove and disprove God's existence as well as to philosophy of religion generally is *Philosophy of Religion: An Anthology of Contemporary Views*, ed. Melville Stewart. An anthology that combines contemporary and classical sources on these matters is *Philosophy of Religion: An Anthology*, ed. Louis Pojman.

# Glossary of Terms

*a posteriori knowledge (or truth)*. Knowledge or truth that is grounded on experience.

*a priori knowledge (or truth)*. Knowledge or truth that is not grounded on experience. Mathematical truth and knowledge are sometimes alleged to be a priori.

*agent causality*. A substance bringing about an event where there are no prior events or conditions that causally necessitated the substance to bring about the event. (Agent causality is typically contrasted with "event causality" in which one event is the cause of another event.)

*avoidability condition*. A condition on moral responsibility that states that a person ought to be held morally responsible only for those actions or states of affairs that the person could have avoided.

*compatibilism*. The theory that one and the same action can be both free and causally necessitated.

*counterfactual of freedom*. An assertion about what a being would have freely chosen to do had the situation been other than it actually was. It is called a counterfactual of freedom because it speculates about what a *free* being would have done had the *facts* been *counter* to what they actually were.

*deliberative conditionals*. An assertion about what a free being would freely do in circumstances that have not yet obtained but may obtain in the future.

*determinism*. The theory that everything that happens is the inevitable causal product of antecedent events and states of affairs.

*event causality.* See *agent causality.*

*evidential problem of evil.* The contention that the evil in the universe renders God's nonexistence more likely than God's existence.

*hard determinism.* The view that all actions and events are causally necessitated and thus are not free.

*instrumentalism.* A theory in the philosophy of science that maintains that scientific theories are mere instruments or tools for predicting future experiences.

*libertarianism.* The view that some human actions are free where the account of their freedom includes (but is not necessarily limited to) the contention that they are not causally necessitated.

*logical problem of evil.* The contention that it is logically contradictory to believe in God's existence and the existence of evil in the universe.

*middle knowledge.* Knowledge concerning what free beings would do under circumstances that are not currently actual. Knowing counterfactuals of freedom or deliberative conditionals would both be cases of middle knowledge.

*moral evil.* Misfortunes that human beings intentionally inflict upon themselves or upon others.

*natural evil.* Misfortunes that the natural order inflicts on human beings and other sentient animals.

*omnibenevolent.* All-good.

*omnipotent.* All-powerful.

*omniscient.* All-knowing.

*ownership condition.* A condition on moral responsibility that states that a person should be held responsible for an action or state of affairs only if the person is the causal source of the action.

*soft determinism.* See *compatibilism.*

*state of affairs.* A way things are; a fact of the matter.

# Bibliography

Adams, Marilyn McCord and Robert Adams, eds. *The Problem of Evil*. Oxford: Oxford University Press, 1990.

Adams, Marilyn McCord. "Horrendous Evils and the Goodness of God." In *The Problem of Evil*, ed. Marilyn M. Adams and Robert Adams, 209–221.

Adams, Robert. "Middle Knowledge and the Problem of Evil," in *The Problem of Evil*, ed. Marilyn M. Adams and Robert Adams, pp. 110–125.

———. "The Problem of Evil." In *Alvin Plantinga*, ed. James Tomberlin and Peter Van Inwagen, 225–255.

Alston, William. "The Inductive Argument from Evil." In *The Evidential Argument from Evil*, ed. Daniel Howard-Snyder, 97–125.

Aquinas, Saint Thomas. *Summa Theologiae* 3 vols. Trans. The Fathers of the English Dominican Province. New York: Benziger Brothers, 1947. (Designated by ST throughout.)

Augustine of Hippo, Saint. *City of God*. Trans. Henry Bettenson. New York: Penguin Books, 1984.

———. *The Confessions*. Trans. Henry Chadwick. Oxford: Oxford University Press, 1991.

Ayer, A.J. *Philosophical Essays*. New York: Macmillan, 1954.

Beversluis, John. *C. S. Lewis and the Search for Rational Religion*. Grand Rapids, MI: Eerdmans, 1985.

Bourke, Vernon J., ed. *The Essential Augustine*. New York: New American Library, 1964.

Breathnach, Sarah Ban. *Simple Abundance: A Daybook of Comfort and Joy*. New York: Warner Books, 1995.

Castell, A., D. Borchert, and A. Zucker. *An Introduction to Modern Philosophy: Examining the Human Condition*. New York: Macmillan, 1988.

Chisholm, Roderick. "The Defeat of Good and Evil." In *The Problem of Evil*, ed. Marilyn M. Adams and Robert Adams, 53–68.

———. "Responsibilty and Avoidability." In *Determinism and Freedom in the Age of Modern Science*, ed. Sidney Hook.

Collodi, C. *Pinocchio*. Adapted by Dick Kelsey in *Walt Disney's Treasury*. New York: Golden Press, 1953.

Descartes, René. *Oeuvres de Descartes*. 12 vols. Ed. Ch. Adam and P. Tannery. Paris: Vriu, 1964–1976. (Designated by AT throughout.)

———. *The Philosophical Writing of Descartes*. 3 vols. Trans. John Cottingham et al. Cambridge: Cambridge University Press, 1989. (Designated by CSM throughout.)

Dostoyevsky, Fyodor. *The Brothers Karamazov*. Trans. Constance Garnett. New York: Random House, 1955.

Ducasse, C.J. "Determinism, Freedom, and Responsibility." In *Determinism and Freedom in the Age of Modern Science*, ed. Sidney Hook, 160–169.

Duhem, Pierre. *The Aim and Structure of Physical Theory.* Trans. Philip Weiner. New York: Atheneum, 1977.

Earman, John. *A Primer on Determinism.* Dordrecht, Holland: D. Reidel, 1986.

Edwards, Paul. "Hard and Soft Determinism." In *Determination and Freedom in the Age of Modern Science*, ed. S. Hook, 117–125.

Eliade, Mircea, ed. *Encyclopedia of Religion.* New York: Macmillan, 1993.

Eldredge, Niles. *Life in the Balance: Humanity and the Biodiversity Crisis.* Princeton: Princeton University Press, 1998.

Frankfurt, Harry. "Alternate Possibilities and Moral Responsibility." *The Journal of Philosophy* 66, no. 23 (December 1969): 829–839.

Gould, Stephen Jay. *Rocks of Ages: Science and Religion in the Fullness of Life.* New York: Random House, 1999.

Gourevitch, Philip. *We Wish to Inform You That Tomorrow We Will Be Killed with Our Families.* New York: Farrar, Straus and Giroux, 1998.

Grahame, Kenneth. *The Wind in the Willows.* New York, Charles Scribner's Sons. 1961.

Hancock, Curtis, and Brendan Sweetman. *Truth and Religious Belief: Conversations on Philosophy of Religion.* Armonk, NY: M.E. Sharpe, 1998.

Hick, John. *Evil and the God of Love.* New York: Harper and Row, 1966.

Hook, Sidney, ed. *Determinism and Freedom in the Age of Modern Science.* New York: Macmillan, 1974.

Howard-Snyder, Daniel. *The Evidential Argument from Evil.* Bloomington: Indiana University Press, 1966.

Hume, David. *Dialogues and Natural History of Religion.* Oxford: Oxford University Press, 1993.

———. *An Enquiry Concerning Human Understanding.* Indianapolis: Hackett, 1977.

Imamura, Akitune. *Theoretical and Applied Seismology.* Trans. D. Kennedy. Tokyo: Maruzen, 1937.

Kane, Robert. "Responsibility, Luck, and Chance: Reflections on Free Will and Indeterminism." *The Journal of Philosophy* 96, no. 5 (May 1999): 217–240.

Kant, Immanuel. *The Critique of Pure Reason.* Trans. Werner S. Pluhar. Indianapolis: Hackett, 1996.

———. *Grounding for a Metaphysics of Morals.* Trans. James W. Ellington. Indianapolis: Hackett, 1981.

Klaidman, Daniel and Mark Hosenball. "The Inside Story of Flight 990." *Newsweek,* November 29, 1999.

Klein, Martha. *Determinism, Blameworthiness and Deprivation.* Oxford: Oxford University Press, 1990.

Latus, Andrew. "Moral and Epistemic Luck." *Journal of Philosophical Research* 25 (2000).

Lewis, C.S. *The Problem of Pain.* New York: Macmillan, 1962.

Maclean, Norman. *Young Men and Fire.* Chicago: University of Chicago Press, 1992.

Mackie, J.L. "Evil and Omnipotence." *Mind* 64 (1955): 200–212. Also in Adams and Adams, *The Problem of Evil*.

Melville, Herman. *Moby Dick.* New York: W.W. Norton, 1967.

Mill, John Stuart. *Utilitarianism, On Liberty and Essay on Bentham.* Ed. Mary Warnock. New York: World, 1971.

Orwell, George. *The Road to Wigan Pier.* New York: Harcourt. Brace, 1958.

Plantinga, Alvin. "God, Evil, and the Metaphysics of Freedom." In *The Problem of Evil*, ed. Adams and Adams, 83–109.

————. *The Nature of Necessity.* Oxford: Oxford University Press, 1974.

————. "Self-Profile." In *Alvin Plantinga*, ed. James Tomberlin and Peter van Inwagen, 3–97.

Plato. *Five Dialogues.* Trans. G.M.A. Grube. Indianapolis: Hackett, 1981.

Pojman, Louis. *Philosophy of Religion: An Anthology.* Belmont, CA: Wadsworth, 1998.

Reichenbach, Bruce. *Evil and a Good God.* New York: Fordham University Press, 1982.

Rowe, William. "The Problem of Evil and Some Varieties of Atheism." In *The Problem of Evil*, ed. Adams and Adams, 126–137.

Stace, Walter. *Religion and the Modern Mind.* New York: Harper and Row, 1952.

Stewart, Melville Y., ed. *Philosophy of Religion: An Anthology of Contemporary Views.* Sudbury, MA: Jones and Bartlett, 1996.

Tomberlin, James and Peter van Inwagen, eds. *Alvin Plantinga.* Dordrecht, Holland: D. Reidel, 1985.

Van Inwagen, Peter. *An Essay on Free Will.* Oxford: Clarendon Press, 1983.

Zucker, Arthur. *Introduction to the Philosophy of Science.* Upper Saddle River, NJ: Prentice Hall, 1996.

# Index

# About the Author

**James Petrik** is associate professor of philosophy at Ohio University in Athens, Ohio. He is the author of *Descartes' Theory of the Will* (1992) and has published articles on the philosophy of religion and early modern philosophy.